PASTA SAUCES

PASTA SAUCES

Over 200 of the best recipes

hamlyn

An Hachette Livre UK Company
www.hachettelivre.co.uk

First published in Great Britain in 2007 by Hamlyn,
a division of Octopus Publishing Group Ltd,
2–4 Heron Quays, London E14 4JP
www.octopusbooks.co.uk

ISBN: 978-0-600-61699-3

A CIP catalogue record for this book is available
from the British Library

Printed and bound in China

10 9 8 7 6 5 4 3 2

Notes
This book includes dishes made with nuts and nut derivatives.
It is advisable for those with known allergic reactions to
nuts and nut derivatives and those who may be potentially
vulnerable to these allergies, such as pregnant and nursing
mothers, invalids, the elderly, babies and children, to avoid
dishes made with nuts and nut oils. It is also prudent to check
the labels of preprepared ingredients for the possible inclusion
of nut derivatives.

The Department of Health advises that eggs should not be
consumed raw. This book contains some dishes made with
raw or lightly cooked eggs. It is prudent for more vulnerable
people such as pregnant and nursing mothers, invalids, the
elderly, babies and young children to avoid uncooked or lightly
cooked dishes made with eggs.

Both metric and imperial measurements are given for the
recipes. Use one set of measures only, not a mixture of both.

Ovens should be preheated to the specified temperature.
If using a fan-assisted oven, follow the manufacturer's
instructions for adjusting the time and temperature.
Grills should also be preheated.

Fresh herbs should be used unless otherwise stated.

Figures given for preparation and cooking times ('Prep' and
'Cook') are given in minutes.

contents

introduction

The pleasure of pasta

When asked to list their favourite foods, the chances are that many people would put pasta at the top. It has become something of a staple in recent times, and with good reason. Apart from being a source of important carbohydrates in our diet, it's also economical, can be quick to prepare, and you don't need to be an accomplished cook to make a pasta meal. However, perhaps its most endearing quality is its versatility. With literally hundreds of different pasta varieties available and endless ideas for accompanying sauces, it's very difficult to tire of pasta as a meal option. In fact, whatever your favourite flavour combinations and ingredients, you're bound to find a sauce that reflects this.

As you will see later on in the book, pasta sauces don't need to be particularly elaborate or full of unusual ingredients. In fact, some of the more famous Italian sauces are made up of just a handful of ingredients: the key is quality not quantity. For example, spaghetti can be served with nothing more than a drizzle of really good-quality olive oil, some chopped garlic and a scattering of freshly chopped basil. Pasta sauces can be quite adaptable too, so once you've mastered some of the recipes you might want to experiment for yourself, maybe adding a little extra chorizo or an extra handful of grated Parmesan cheese as the mood takes you. As with all things Italian, cooking pasta comes down to enjoyment. From preparing the ingredients to sitting down and eating the food, the whole experience should be a laid-back and pleasurable one.

Family favourite

Both fresh and dried pasta are very quick to cook, so pasta really is a great choice for fast and easy family meals. It's something that parents and kids can sit down and enjoy together, and even the fussiest children are usually pacified by a plate of simple spaghetti Bolognese. Most pasta sauces can be prepared in advance and then kept in the fridge or freezer until needed, which is great if you've had the busiest day in history and really don't fancy the idea of getting home and preparing a meal from scratch. Just cook the pasta, reheat the sauce and dinner is served – a hot, homemade and delicious dinner at that. If your children have a phobia of vegetables, pasta can be a great way to top up their five-a-day without the usual tantrums. Coarser sauces can be whizzed up in the blender to produce a smooth consistency that will look and taste like nothing more than an innocent tomato sauce. They'll never be able to detect the other nutritious goodies, and you'll all be happy.

An economic option

Another reason for the huge popularity of pasta is that you can enjoy a really nutritious and filling meal without breaking the bank. This has made pasta something of a favourite with students, although the days of pasta with a can of tuna, some mayonnaise and a spoon seem to have been left behind for slightly more lofty intentions in the kitchen. With many students arriving at college with little more than a cursory knowledge of the workings of a kitchen, worried parents have armed them with expedition-sized rations of pasta in the belief that even the most culinary challenged among them won't go hungry. While it's true that most student sauces will initially start life in a can or jar, there's often a quick progression to the homemade variety, and pasta is the perfect training ground for cooking experiments.

Although pasta might be an economical option, it's also just as likely to be seen on the menus of top restaurants as in your local pub or café. There's a real art to making homemade pasta, as the results should be delicate without breaking up while cooking, and it's a chance for chefs to get really creative with fillings for ravioli and sauces that will complement various types of pasta.

Viva Italia

Pasta has rather an illustrious history, and although we almost always associate it with the cuisine of Italy, there are references to similar dishes being eaten in other countries. Some credit the traveller Marco Polo with the introduction of pasta to Italy, while others believe that the Arab invasions saw the first dried pasta being introduced to the country, along with other ingredients that were subsequently absorbed into the local cuisine.

No matter how it arrived, there's no denying the fact that the Italians got truly creative with this practical and nutritious food and it quickly became a staple. Because dried pasta has such a long shelf life, it became a favourite provision for lengthy sea voyages, and this also helped it to gain popularity further afield. Techniques and machinery were developed to make the process of producing pasta less labour intensive, and these resulted in the increase in the variety of shapes and types of pasta. The introduction of tomatoes into Europe helped seal the future of pasta because they provided the perfect base for sauces.

Types of pasta

Pasta comes in all shapes and sizes and can be made from a variety of different ingredients, including special ranges for people who suffer from a number of food intolerances. Most dried pastas are made simply from flour and water, which means they have a long shelf life. Durum wheat is usually the main ingredient.

❋ Egg pastas

There are some dried pastas that contain egg products, but it's generally fresh varieties that are made with eggs. They add colour and flavour to the pasta, as well as helping the ingredients to bind and stay together during the cooking process.

❋ Wholemeal

Many pasta shapes are also now available in wholemeal varieties. As with other wholemeal products, this means the carbohydrates have a slower release rate, which is good for maintaining a constant energy level in the body.

❋ Flavoured pasta

Spinach and tomato are two popular flavours for pasta, and you will often see fresh tagliatelle in these varieties.

❋ Gluten-free

There are a number of gluten-free pasta ranges on the market. They have been specially developed for coeliacs but offer a good comparative taste and texture with regular pasta.

Pasta varieties

Penne

This popular tube-shaped pasta is cut on the diagonal and has ridges, which help sauces to cling to individual pieces of pasta. It goes particularly well with chunky, tomato-based sauces.

Macaroni

These are small tubes without ridges and they are probably best known as the star ingredient in macaroni cheese.

Farfalle

These little bow shapes are great for pasta salads or with vegetable sauces.

Fusilli

This versatile pasta is spiral-shaped. It goes well with all kinds of sauces or can be used to make salads.

Orecchiette

This is becoming increasingly popular. Translated from Italian as 'little ears', it's a robust pasta that works well in baked recipes or with hearty meat sauces.

Spaghetti

These long strands are most often combined with the famous Bolognese Sauce (see page 28), but they also go well with shellfish and creamy sauces.

Tagliatelle

This wide, flat pasta is available in spinach and tomato varieties as well. Quick Carbonara Sauce (see page 232) is a popular accompaniment, but any creamy sauce will do the trick.

Ravioli

These stuffed pasta shapes come with a variety of fillings, from cheese to meat. Freshly made ravioli is often served as a starter in restaurants.

How to cook pasta

The key to cooking pasta is timing. Different varieties take a longer or shorter time to cook, so always check the instructions on the packet. However, you shouldn't simply rely on this, and it's a good idea to try a piece of pasta before you decide to dish up. You also don't necessarily need to stick to the exact measurements for the pasta. As you get more confident you'll work out your own specific requirements for different pasta varieties with different sauces. However, you also need to think about whether you're preparing a starter or main course; a light meal or a substantial dinner; and, of course, the appetites of you and your guests! Here's a step-by-step cooking guide:

1 Pour boiling water into a large saucepan and place over a high heat to bring back to the boil. Add a pinch of salt to the water.

2 Measure out the required amount of pasta and add it to the pan. Add the pasta to the boiling water. Give it a quick stir because it can sometimes stick to the bottom of the pan.

3 Cook according to the packet instructions but as the time approaches, start removing and trying pieces of pasta until you're happy that it's cooked. You want your pasta to retain its shape and have a little bite to it (al dente).

4 Drain the pasta immediately, return to the hot pan (off the heat) and stir in the sauce. It's important to do this and mix well before serving, as pasta will stick together once it's drained.

Cooking fresh pasta

Fresh pasta cooks a lot more quickly than dried and it's not as robust, so avoid stirring it during cooking. Most fresh pastas take no more than a few minutes to cook so you really need to keep an eye on the time. Overcooked pasta will become very soggy and lose its shape (and the filling if it's a stuffed pasta). As with dried pasta, cook in a large saucepan of boiling, salted water and drain thoroughly once cooked. Again, you should add the sauce immediately and mix well before serving.

 ## Top tips

* Use the biggest pan that you have – pasta needs plenty of space to move when it's cooking.
* Always add pasta to boiling water, never to cold water.
* If you're not mixing the sauce into the pasta straight away or you're making a pasta salad, add a little olive oil to the drained pasta and mix in well to stop the pasta sticking together.

 ## Matching pasta with sauce

With such a dizzying array of pasta shapes on the market, it can be a little confusing when it comes to matching up your choice of pasta with a suitable sauce. Most recipes will advise you of the best pasta to use with the particular recipe; however, it's good to know which types of sauces naturally complement particular types of pasta. That way, if you've run out of the required shape, you might be able to substitute it for something else in the store-cupboard. The table below is a basic guide to which sauces work best with which types of pasta.

Pasta type	Example	Sauce
tubes	penne, rigatoni	chunky sauces
long and thin	spaghetti, linguine	olive oil and herb-based sauces
shapes	farfalle, conchiglie	rough or textured sauces

Store-cupboard staples

There are certain ingredients that appear in many recipes in this book and it's a good idea to keep stocked up with these basics if you're a pasta fan. Always buy the best quality ingredients that your budget allows because this will make all the difference to the taste of the finished dish.

 Tomatoes

These are an absolute staple when cooking pasta sauces. Different recipes call for different tomatoes but it's good to have a stock of both fresh and canned tomatoes. If you have time opt for fresh, but you'll need to skin them first. To do this, fill a large saucepan with water and bring to the boil. Make a cross at the base of each tomato and plunge them into the water for 30 seconds. Remove the tomatoes with a slotted spoon then plunge them into cold water. Drain them well and the skins will then peel off very easily.

 Garlic

This makes an appearance in most pasta sauce recipes and, indeed, throughout Italian cuisine. Always use fresh garlic – don't be tempted by the jars of crushed cloves. You will usually need either to slice the cloves finely or crush them, which you can do with the base of a rolling pin or the side of a knife.

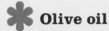 **Olive oil**

Choose good-quality extra virgin oil, unless the recipe states otherwise. Like wine, olive oil varies greatly in quality and taste and you'll appreciate the difference in the taste of the sauce.

 Herbs

Again, these have a central role to play in many pasta sauces. Always try to use fresh herbs, as the flavour is infinitely superior. Basil, oregano and parsley are three of the herbs that you'll see appear in many recipes so keep a stock of these in your kitchen. Better still, grow your own!

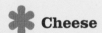 **Cheese**

Parmesan, pecorino, mascarpone and mozzarella are four cheeses that have star turns in a number of recipes in this book. Freshly grated Parmesan is a must and choose buffalo mozzarella if it's available.

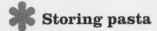 **Storing pasta**

Dried pasta is a wonderful store-cupboard staple as it lasts for years – literally! If the pasta is egg-based it should last for up to two years, while non egg-based varieties will last for up to three years. Always check individual packaging for exact dates. Once cooked, you can keep pasta in the refrigerator for three days. Drizzle a little oil over it and mix through before storing it. This will stop the pasta from sticking together.

Bought fresh pasta varies considerably, and how long it will keep will often depend on whether it's a stuffed pasta and on what the filling is made from. Again, you should always check the date on the packet and keep all fresh pasta in the fridge. It's often possible to freeze fresh pasta, and many varieties can be cooked directly from frozen.

Fish stock

25 g (1 oz) **butter**

3 **shallots**, roughly chopped

1 small **leek**, roughly chopped

1 **celery stick** or piece of **fennel**, roughly chopped

1 kg (2 lb) **white fish** or **shellfish bones, heads and trimmings**

150 ml (¼ pint) dry **white wine**

several sprigs of **parsley**

½ **lemon**, sliced

1 teaspoon **black peppercorns** or **white peppercorns**

1 litre (1¾ pints) **water**

PREP

10

COOK

30

1 litre

1¾ pints

MAKES

Do not use oily fish to make stock because it will make it greasy and give it an overpowering flavour. Fish stock requires less cooking than meat stocks, so take care that you do not overcook it or you will spoil the flavour.

1 Melt the butter in a large, heavy-based saucepan until bubbling.

2 Add all the vegetables and cook over a moderate heat for 5 minutes or until softened but not browned. Add the fish bones, heads and trimmings, wine, parsley, lemon, peppercorns and measured water.

3 Bring to the boil, skimming off the scum that rises to the surface. Reduce the heat and simmer the stock for 20 minutes.

4 Strain, cover and leave to cool. Chill in the refrigerator overnight, then remove and discard the layer of fat that will have set on the surface. Store in the refrigerator for up to 24 hours or freeze immediately.

Chicken stock

10
PREP

120
COOK

1
litre

1¾
pints

MAKES

Never throw away the carcass of a chicken. Cooked or raw, it makes a fabulous stock and the basis of so many good soups. Gather up all the bones, skin and pan scrapings from a roast. Alternatively, if you are using a raw carcass, cook it for about 30 minutes in a hot oven first until browned.

1 Pack the chicken carcass into a large, heavy-based saucepan, crushing the bones if necessary to make it fit. Add the trimmings, vegetables, bay leaves and peppercorns. Just cover with cold water.

2 Bring slowly to the boil, skimming off the scum that rises to the surface. Reduce the heat and simmer very gently for 1½–2 hours.

3 Strain, cover and leave to cool. Chill in the refrigerator overnight, then remove and discard the layer of fat that will have set on the surface. Store in the refrigerator for up to 4 days or freeze immediately.

1 large **chicken carcass**, including any trimmings, such as the neck, heart and gizzard if available (but not the liver)

1 **onion**, roughly chopped

1 large **carrot**, roughly chopped

several **bay leaves**

1 teaspoon **black peppercorns**

Beef stock

1.75 kg (3½ lb) **beef bones**, chopped into 8 cm (3 inch) pieces

2 **onions**, quartered

2 **carrots**, chopped

2 **celery sticks**, chopped

2 **tomatoes**, chopped

4 litres (7 pints) **water**

10 sprigs of **parsley**

4 sprigs of **thyme**

2 **bay leaves**

8 **black peppercorns**

15
PREP

300
COOK

2
litres

3½
pints

MAKES

When you buy beef, remember to get the bones as well and ask your butcher to cut them into manageable pieces. You can use cheaper cuts of beef and trimmings instead, but that's more expensive than using bones.

1 Put the bones in a large roasting tin and roast in a preheated oven, 230°C (450°F), Gas Mark 8, for 30 minutes or until lightly browned and the fat and juices run, turning occasionally. Add all the vegetables, spoon over the fat from the tin and roast, stirring occasionally, for a further 30 minutes.

2 Transfer the bones and vegetables to a large, heavy-based saucepan. Pour off the fat from the tin and add 150 ml (¼ pint) of the measured water. Set over a low heat and bring to the boil, scraping up any sediment. Pour into the saucepan. Add the remaining water.

3 Bring to the boil, skimming off the scum that rises to the surface. Add the herbs and peppercorns. Partially cover, then reduce the heat and simmer for 4 hours.

4 Strain, cover and leave to cool. Chill in the refrigerator overnight, then remove and discard the layer of fat that will have set on the surface. Store in the refrigerator for up to 4 days or freeze immediately.

Vegetable stock

15

PREP

You can use any combination of vegetables that you like, but make sure that they are fresh. Always include onions, but avoid any with strong flavours, such as cabbage, and starchy ones, such as potatoes, which will make the stock cloudy. In many of the recipes you can use chicken stock instead.

1 Melt the butter in a large, heavy-based saucepan, add all the vegetables and stir well to coat, then cover and cook over a low heat for 10 minutes.

2 Stir in all the herbs and add the measured water. Bring to the boil, then reduce the heat, cover and simmer for 15 minutes.

3 Strain the stock, cover and leave to cool. Chill in the refrigerator overnight. Store the stock in the refrigerator for up to 2 days or freeze immediately.

30

COOK

600 ml

1 pint

MAKES

50 g (2 oz) **butter**

2 **onions**, chopped

2 **leeks**, thinly sliced

2 **carrots**, chopped

2 **celery sticks**, chopped

1 **fennel bulb**, chopped

1 sprig of **thyme**

1 sprig of **marjoram**

1 sprig of **fennel**

4 sprigs of **parsley**

900 ml (1½ pints) **water**

classics

Pesto

50 g (2 oz) **basil**, including stalks

50 g (2 oz) **pine nuts**

65 g (2½ oz) **Parmesan cheese**, freshly grated

2 **garlic cloves**, chopped

125 ml (4 fl oz) **olive oil**

salt and **pepper**

5

PREP

0

COOK

4

SERVES

fresh

Making pesto traditionally with a pestle and mortar fills the air with the wonderful fragrance of crushed basil leaves, but it is more time consuming than the food processor method used here. Freshly made pesto makes a wonderful pasta sauce.

1 Tear the basil into pieces and put it into a food processor with the pine nuts, Parmesan and garlic.

2 Blend lightly in the food processor until the nuts and cheese are broken into small pieces, scraping the mixture down from the sides of the bowl if necessary.

3 Add the olive oil and a little salt and blend to a thick paste. It can be kept in a lidded jar, covered with a layer of olive oil, for up to 5 days.

Pesto trapanese

12

PREP

This recipe is a legacy of the Arab domination of Sicily. The Arabs brought almonds to the island, and this pesto comes from Trapani, where they first settled.

0

COOK

1 Place all of the ingredients in a food processor and blend until they are smooth. Alternatively, finely chop the tomatoes, garlic, basil and almonds by hand, and stir in the olive oil to give a chunkier sauce.

2 Season to taste with salt and pepper, garnish with the extra basil leaves. It can be kept in a lidded jar, covered with a layer of olive oil, for up to 5 days.

4–6

SERVES

easy

3 ripe **tomatoes**

4 **garlic cloves**

50 g (2 oz) **basil leaves**, plus extra to garnish

125 g (4 oz) **blanched almonds**, toasted

150 ml (¼ pint) **olive oil**

salt and **pepper**

500 g (1 lb) minced **beef**

½ large **onion**, very finely chopped

1 **garlic clove**, crushed

1 teaspoon chopped **oregano**

1 teaspoon **dried mixed herbs**

50 g (2 oz) fresh **breadcrumbs**

1 **egg**, beaten

2 tablespoons **olive oil**

salt and **pepper**

parsley sprigs, to garnish

SAUCE:

1 **onion**

400 g (13 oz) can **plum tomatoes**

600 ml (1 pint) **beef stock** (see page 20)

2 tablespoons **tomato purée**

1 tablespoon **red wine vinegar**

1 teaspoon chopped **oregano**

1 teaspoon **dried mixed herbs**

1 teaspoon **caster sugar**

20

PREP

30

COOK

4–5

SERVES

meaty

Meatball sauce

These herby beef meatballs and rich tomato sauce are wonderful served with spaghetti or any other long, thin pasta as an alternative to a Bolognese sauce.

1 Put all the sauce ingredients in a blender and work to a purée. Transfer to a pan and season. Bring to the boil, stirring. Reduce the heat, cover and simmer, stirring occasionally, while making the meatballs.

2 Place the beef in a bowl and combine it with the onion, garlic, herbs, breadcrumbs and egg. Season to taste. Knead for about 5 minutes until the meat is sticky. Shape into about 50 very small balls.

3 Heat the oil in a nonstick frying pan and fry the meatballs in batches for 5–7 minutes until they are brown on all sides. Remove them and place them on kitchen paper to drain.

4 Add the meatballs to the sauce. Cover the pan and cook very gently for about 20 minutes, shaking the pan occasionally. Garnish with parsley sprigs.

Fresh coriander sauce

This creamy combination of the summery fragrance of coriander and pine nuts with smooth-textured cream cheese produces a simple yet delicious sauce.

1 Set some of the coriander leaves aside for the garnish and chop the rest finely. Place them in a mortar with the pine nuts and crush with a pestle. Alternatively, combine the leaves and nuts in a bowl and use the end of a rolling pin to crush the mixture.

2 Heat the oil in a saucepan. Add the shallots and fry for 2 minutes, stirring constantly. Lower the heat and stir in the coriander mixture with the cream cheese and then the milk or cream. Add salt and pepper to taste. Bring to the boil, then reduce the heat and simmer for 2 minutes or until thoroughly heated through.

3 Garnish with the reserved coriander leaves, then serve.

5

PREP

5

COOK

4

SERVES

herby

1 large bunch of fresh **coriander**, leaves stripped from stalks

50 g (2 oz) **pine nuts**

1½ tablespoons **olive oil**

125 g (4 oz) **shallots**

250 g (8 oz) half-fat **cream cheese**

125 ml (4 fl oz) **milk** or **single cream**

salt and **pepper**

25 g (1 oz) **butter**

2 tablespoons **olive oil**

1 **onion**, finely chopped

2 **celery sticks**, finely chopped

2 **garlic cloves**, crushed

500 g (1 lb) lean minced **beef**

200 g (7 oz) spicy **Italian sausages**, skinned

300 ml (½ pint) **red wine** or **white wine**

400 g (13 oz) can **chopped tomatoes**

1 teaspoon **caster sugar**

2 **bay leaves**

1 teaspoon **dried oregano**

2 tablespoons **sun-dried tomato paste**

salt and **pepper**

15

PREP

75

COOK

6

SERVES

meaty

Bolognese sauce

Combining Italian-style spicy sausages with the more familiar minced beef gives this sauce a rich meaty flavour that is reminiscent of the traditional sauce served in Bologna. Allow time for long, gentle cooking to tenderize the meat and let the flavours mingle.

1 Melt the butter with the oil in a large heavy-based saucepan and gently fry the onion and celery for 5 minutes.

2 Add the garlic, beef and the skinned sausages, and cook until they are lightly coloured, breaking up the mince and sausages with a wooden spoon.

3 Add the wine and allow it to bubble for 1–2 minutes until slightly evaporated. Add the tomatoes, sugar, bay leaves, oregano, tomato paste and a little salt and pepper and bring just to the boil. Reduce the heat to its lowest setting, cover the pan with a lid and cook for about 1 hour, stirring occasionally, until thick and pulpy.

Lentil bolognese sauce

Unlike some types of lentils, green lentils do not need lengthy pre-soaking: simply rinse, then cook. This speeds up this vegetarian version of the classic Bolognese sauce.

10

PREP

55

COOK

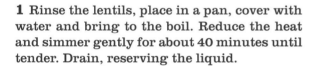

4

SERVES

hearty

250 g (8 oz) **whole green lentils**

2 teaspoons **vegetable oil**

2 **onions**, chopped

2 **garlic cloves**, crushed

2 **celery sticks**, chopped

2 **carrots**, finely diced

2 tablespoons **tomato purée**

salt and **pepper**

1 Rinse the lentils, place in a pan, cover with water and bring to the boil. Reduce the heat and simmer gently for about 40 minutes until tender. Drain, reserving the liquid.

2 Meanwhile, heat the oil in a large saucepan, add the onions and cook for 5 minutes, until soft, then add the garlic, celery and carrots. Cook the vegetables, covered, for 15 minutes or until tender.

3 Stir in the lentils, tomato purée, salt and pepper and a little of the reserved lentil cooking liquid to make a thick, soft consistency. Bring to the boil, then reduce the heat and simmer the sauce for about 10 minutes, adding more liquid if necessary.

1 large **aubergine**, diced

1 tablespoon **olive oil**

2 **onions**, chopped

2 **garlic cloves**, chopped

400 g (13 oz) can
chopped tomatoes

2 teaspoons chopped
basil

salt and **pepper**

40

PREP

25

COOK

4

SERVES

hearty

Sicilienne sauce

Onion, garlic, aubergine and tomato are cooked together here to make a hearty, warming sauce that is also incredibly economical. Serve with freshly grated Parmesan or pecorino to add some protein.

1 Place the diced aubergine in a colander, sprinkle with salt and leave for 30 minutes to remove any bitter taste. Rinse in cold water and dry well with kitchen paper.

2 Heat the oil in a saucepan, add the onion, garlic and aubergine and cook for 2–3 minutes. Add the tomatoes and their juice, together with the basil, and season to taste with salt and pepper. Bring to the boil then reduce the heat and simmer for 15–20 minutes.

Buongustaio sauce

15

PREP

22

COOK

4

SERVES

thick

1 tablespoon **olive oil**

1 large **onion**, finely chopped

2 **garlic cloves**, finely chopped

1 **aubergine**, peeled and diced

125 g (4 oz) **mushrooms**, sliced

400 g (13 oz) can **chopped tomatoes**

sprig of **sage**

salt and **pepper**

Although similar to the Sicilienne Sauce opposite, the addition of mushrooms to the mixture changes the flavour considerably. Serve with bucatini, which is a long pasta, not unlike spaghetti, but with a hole down the middle, like very long, thin macaroni.

1 Heat the oil in a saucepan, add the onion, garlic and aubergine and cook for 5 minutes, then add the mushrooms and tomatoes, plus the juice from the can. Add the sage and a little salt and pepper.

2 Bring the sauce to the boil, then reduce the heat, cover the pan and cook gently for 15 minutes. Remove the sage before serving.

125 g (4 oz) frozen **peas**

50 g (2 oz) **butter**

250 g (8 oz) **button mushrooms**, thinly sliced

200 ml (7 fl oz) **single cream**

125 g (4 oz) piece of lean cooked **ham**, thinly sliced

125 g (4 oz) **Parmesan cheese**, freshly grated

salt

10

PREP

8

COOK

4

SERVES

tasty

Ciociara-style sauce

This sauce is ideal served with the thin green and white ribbons of fresh pasta, which are similar to fettuccine, known as *paglia e fieno* ('straw and hay').

1 Place the peas in a pan of salted boiling water and cook according to the packet instructions until just tender.

2 Meanwhile, melt half of the butter in a frying pan, add the mushrooms and sauté gently until just tender, adding salt to taste.

3 Put the remaining butter in a saucepan with the cream and heat gently without allowing the mixture to boil. Add the mushrooms with their juice, the peas and the cooked ham.

4 Stir a ladle of boiling water and a third of the Parmesan into the sauce, then serve with the remaining cheese.

Syracuse sauce

This rustic sauce is the perfect dish for autumn, when courgettes and peppers are coming to the end of their season and there is a glut to be used up.

PREP **15**

COOK **30**

6

SERVES

rustic

1 Heat a large frying pan and dry-fry the onion and garlic for 3–6 minutes, turning constantly, until soft. Add the courgettes and cook for another 10 minutes.

2 Add the green pepper, tomatoes, olives, anchovies and herbs. Bring to the boil, stirring, then cover the pan and simmer for 10 minutes. Season to taste with salt and pepper and garnish with parsley.

1 large **onion**, sliced

2 **garlic cloves**, crushed

500 g (1 lb) **courgettes**, chopped

1 **green pepper**, cored, deseeded and chopped

400 g (13 oz) can **plum tomatoes**, drained and roughly chopped

125 g (4 oz) pitted **black olives**

3 **anchovy fillets**, finely chopped

1 tablespoon chopped **parsley**

2 teaspoons chopped **marjoram**

salt and **pepper**

few sprigs of **flat leaf parsley**, to garnish

5 tablespoons **olive oil**

1 large **onion**, finely chopped

1 **celery stick**, finely chopped

75 g (3 oz) **pancetta**, cubed

3 **garlic cloves**, crushed

1 hot **red chilli**, deseeded and finely chopped

1 kg (2 lb) ripe, full-flavoured **tomatoes**, skinned (see page 16) and roughly chopped.

salt and **pepper**

15

PREP

40

COOK

4

SERVES

spicy

Amatriciana sauce

This is a good choice for those who like their tomato sauce to have a punchier flavour. If the tomatoes are lacking in flavour, stir in a generous dollop of sun-dried tomato paste.

1 Heat the oil in a large, heavy-based saucepan and gently fry the onion, celery and pancetta, stirring frequently, for 6–8 minutes or until softened. Add the garlic and chilli and fry for a further 2 minutes.

2 Stir in the chopped tomatoes and cook gently, uncovered, stirring frequently, for about 30 minutes or until the sauce is very thick and pulpy. Season to taste with salt and pepper, then serve.

Three-herb sauce

Serve this light, summery dish, fragrant with mixed herbs and garlic, with some multicoloured spaghetti for a beautiful meal to remember.

1 Put all of the ingredients into a food processor or blender and work until smooth, then add salt and pepper to taste.

10

PREP

0

COOK

4

SERVES

herby

3 tablespoons chopped **parsley**

1 tablespoon chopped **tarragon**

2 tablespoons chopped **basil**

1 tablespoon **olive oil**

1 large **garlic clove**, crushed

4 tablespoons **chicken stock** (see page 19)

2 tablespoons dry **white wine**

salt and **pepper**

Pesto genoese

250 g (8 oz) **potatoes**, peeled and thinly sliced

150 g (5 oz) **green beans**

75 g (3 oz) **basil leaves**

25 g (1 oz) **pine nuts**

2 **garlic cloves**, crushed

2 tablespoons freshly grated **Parmesan cheese**, plus extra to serve

1 tablespoon freshly grated **pecorino cheese**

3 tablespoons **olive oil**

salt

15

PREP

15

COOK

4

SERVES

filling

In Genoa, the home of pesto, this aromatic sauce is traditionally cooked with potatoes and green beans before being served with pasta. This might sound unusual, but it is a heavenly combination. Cook the beans for longer if you prefer.

1 Cook the potatoes in a large saucepan of salted boiling water for 10 minutes, then add the beans and cook for a further 5 minutes.

2 Meanwhile, blend the basil, pine nuts and garlic in a food processor until the mixture forms a thick paste. Add the cheeses and process briefly, then, with the motor still running, pour in the oil through the feed tube in a thin, steady stream. Alternatively, use a pestle and mortar.

3 Drain the vegetables, reserving 2 tablespoons of the cooking water. Return the vegetables to the pan and stir in the pesto sauce, adding the reserved water to loosen the mixture. Serve with the extra Parmesan.

Primavera sauce

This sauce uses only seasonally available vegetables, in this case combining those grown in the spring (peas and asparagus) with those grown in the summer (courgettes and tomatoes). Serve with fettucine.

1 Melt the butter in a large saucepan, and gently fry the onion, carrot and celery until soft. Add the peas, tomatoes and courgette, and gently fry for another 5 minutes. Add the asparagus and fry for a further minute.

2 Stir in the cream. Bring to the boil, then reduce the heat and simmer gently until reduced by half. Season to taste with salt and pepper, then garnish with parsley and serve with grated Parmesan.

15
PREP

15
COOK

4
SERVES

fresh

50 g (2 oz) **butter**

1 **onion**, diced

1 **carrot**, diced

1 **celery stick**, diced

100 g (4 oz) shelled **peas**

2 ripe **tomatoes**, skinned (see page 16) and chopped

1 large **courgette**, cut into 1 cm (½ inch) cubes

100 g (4 oz) thin **asparagus**, stalks chopped

300 ml (½ pint) **double cream**

salt and **pepper**

2 tablespoons finely chopped **flat leaf parsley**, to garnish

50 g (2 oz) **Parmesan cheese**, freshly grated, to serve

4–5 **garlic cloves**, peeled

50 g (2 oz) **basil leaves**

pinch of **dried chilli flakes**

150 ml (¼ pint) **olive oil**

6 ripe **tomatoes**, about 750 g (1½ lb), skinned (see page 16) and chopped

125 g (4 oz) **salted ricotta cheese** or **pecorino cheese**, grated, plus extra to serve

salt

Carter's sauce

15

PREP

0

COOK

6

SERVES

rustic

This sauce was a staple food of Sicilian cart drivers, quickly rustled up by the side of the road with a few basic ingredients: tomatoes, garlic, olive oil and salted ricotta, which kept well because it was preserved.

1 Put the garlic, basil, chilli flakes and a pinch of salt into a food processor and work until smooth, then add the oil slowly until the sauce becomes smooth again. Alternatively, use a pestle and mortar. Mix the purée into the chopped tomatoes.

2 Stir half of the cheese into the sauce and sprinkle the remaining cheese on top. Serve with a small bowl of grated cheese handed around separately.

Peperonata sauce

This delicious spaghetti sauce has a fresh, spicy flavour and is perfect for a winter's lunch or supper.

15

PREP

30

COOK

4

SERVES

fresh

1 Heat the oil in a saucepan, add the onion and garlic and cook for 5 minutes.

2 Add the tomatoes with their juice, the tomato purée, oregano and bay leaves. Bring to the boil, reduce the heat then simmer for 10 minutes.

3 Add the peppers and cook for another 10 minutes or until they are just soft. Season to taste. Remove the bay leaves before serving with a bowl of grated Parmesan.

2 tablespoons **olive oil**

3 **onions**, finely chopped

2 **garlic cloves**, finely chopped

400 g (13 oz) can **chopped tomatoes**

1 tablespoon **tomato purée**

1 tablespoon chopped **oregano**

2 **bay leaves**

1 **green pepper**, cored, deseeded and diced

1 **red pepper**, cored, deseeded and diced

salt and **pepper**

freshly grated **Parmesan cheese**, to serve

2 tablespoons **olive oil**

1 **onion**, chopped

2 **garlic cloves**, crushed

2 **carrots**, finely chopped and blanched

2 **red peppers**, cored, deseeded and finely chopped

4 large **tomatoes**, chopped

150 ml (¼ pint) **red wine**

400 g (14 oz) can **chopped tomatoes with herbs**

salt and **pepper**

1 bunch of **basil leaves**, shredded, to garnish

15

PREP

25

COOK

4

SERVES

rustic

Napoletana sauce

Red wine adds punch to this mixed vegetable sauce, bursting with Italian flavours. Serve with farfalle or other similarly sized pasta.

1 Heat the oil in a large frying pan. Add the onion and garlic and fry for about 3 minutes or until softened but not coloured.

2 Add the carrots and red peppers and fry for a further 3 minutes.

3 Stir in the chopped fresh tomatoes with the red wine and canned tomatoes. Season to taste. Bring to the boil, then reduce the heat and simmer, partially covered, for 15 minutes, then garnish with shredded basil leaves.

Sardine, garlic and tomato sauce

Anchovies, garlic and olives create a strong-flavoured, gutsy sauce to combine with fresh sardines. The slow cooking means that all the flavours will meld together wonderfully. Serve with conchiglie.

20 PREP

25 COOK

4 SERVES

gutsy

500 g (1 lb) **fresh sardines**

3 tablespoons **olive oil**

2 small **onions**, finely chopped

6 **garlic cloves**, crushed

250 g (8 oz) ripe **tomatoes**, skinned (see page 16), deseeded and finely chopped, or 250 g (8 oz) can **chopped tomatoes**

4 canned **anchovy fillets** in oil, pounded to a purée with the oil from the can

6 **black olives**, pitted

1 tablespoon **capers**

1 tablespoon **pine nuts**

1 tablespoon chopped **basil**

pepper

1 Remove the heads and tails from the sardines. Open the fish out gently with your fingers and remove the bones. (Do not worry if the fish breaks because it will break during cooking anyway.)

2 Heat the oil in a heavy-based saucepan. Add the onions and cook gently for about 10 minutes, stirring frequently, until they are golden.

3 Add the sardines and garlic and stir to coat the sardines in the oil and onion. Add all the remaining ingredients. Cover the pan and cook gently for 10–15 minutes. Season to taste and serve.

1.5 kg (3 lb) **baby clams**

4 tablespoons **olive oil**

2 **garlic cloves**, crushed

125 ml (4 fl oz) dry **white wine**

75 ml (3 fl oz) **double cream**

large handful of **flat leaf parsley**, chopped

salt and **pepper**

freshly grated **Parmesan cheese**, to serve

15

PREP

10

COOK

4

SERVES

posh

Vongole sauce

In a marked change from gutsy, tomato-based sauces, here is a light and delicate sauce containing clams, garlic, white wine and cream – perfect for a supper party. This sauce is traditionally served with spaghetti.

1 To wash the baby clams, place them in a colander and submerge in a bowl of cold water. Shake vigorously, then lift out the colander and replace with fresh water. Repeat until the clams are clean, then drain well. Check the clams and discard any that are damaged or open.

2 Heat the oil in a large saucepan over a low heat, add the garlic and clams, cover and cook for 3 minutes or until all the clams have opened. Discard any that do not open.

3 Lift the clams out of the pan with a slotted spoon. Remove half of them from their shells and return any liquid to the pan. Set the clams aside.

4 Add the wine and cream to the pan and increase the heat to reduce the sauce a little.

5 Return the clams to the sauce, stir well, bring to the boil, then reduce the heat and simmer for 2 minutes. Add the parsley, season with salt and pepper and mix well. Serve with grated Parmesan.

Anchovy and garlic sauce

10

PREP

If you dislike the saltiness of anchovies, soaking them in a little milk is a good way to cut down on the salty flavour while maintaining all the delicious anchovy taste.

1 Soak the anchovy fillets in a little milk to remove excess salt, then drain.

2 Heat the oil in a saucepan, add the garlic and the anchovies and cook over a moderate heat for a few minutes, then remove the garlic and add the bacon.

3 When the bacon is crisp, add the tomatoes to the pan. Season with salt and pepper and cook over a low heat for about 10 minutes, then add the olives and oregano. Cook for another 10 minutes or until a thick sauce has formed. Serve with grated pecorino.

25

COOK

4

SERVES

tasty

2 **anchovy fillets**

a little **milk**

4 tablespoons **oil**

1 **garlic clove**

50 g (2 oz) **smoked bacon**, rind removed and diced

400 g (13 oz) can **plum tomatoes**, drained and cut into strips

50 g (2 oz) pitted **black olives**, chopped

¼ teaspoon chopped **oregano**

salt and **pepper**

25 g (1 oz) **pecorino cheese**, freshly grated, to serve

2 x 400 g (13 oz) cans **plum tomatoes**, drained

25 g (1 oz) **butter**

1 **onion**, finely chopped

125 g (4 oz) **streaky bacon**, rind removed and diced

2 **garlic cloves**, finely chopped

1–2 **red chillies**, finely chopped

1 tablespoon chopped **oregano**

1 tablespoon chopped **thyme**

salt and **pepper**

1 tablespoon chopped **parsley**, to garnish

125 g (4 oz) **Parmesan cheese**, freshly grated, to serve

10

PREP

40

COOK

4

SERVES

spicy

Herby all'arrabiata sauce

Red chillies add a kick to this tomato and bacon sauce, flavoured with oregano, thyme and parsley. Serve with penne pasta for a popular lunch dish.

1 Purée the tomatoes in a food processor or blender, then set aside until required.

2 Melt the butter in a large saucepan over a moderate heat. Add the onion and bacon and cook, stirring, for 5 minutes. Add the garlic and chillies, then cook, stirring occasionally, for a further 5 minutes or until the onion is tender.

3 Add the tomatoes, oregano and thyme and season the sauce to taste with salt and pepper. Cover the sauce, bring to the boil, then reduce the heat and simmer for about 30 minutes. Garnish with the parsley and serve with the grated Parmesan.

Puttanesca sauce

This intense Italian tomato sauce has plenty of flavours, such as black olives, anchovies and capers. Thick and rich, it's great tossed with almost any pasta, especially spaghetti, for a deliciously quick supper dish.

1 Heat the oil in a saucepan over a moderate heat, add the onions and cook gently for 5 minutes until softened.

2 Add the garlic and anchovies and cook for about 3 minutes until the anchovies completely disintegrate.

3 Stir in the tomatoes, olives, capers and oregano, and season to taste with salt and pepper. Bring to the boil, then reduce the heat and simmer the sauce gently for about 20 minutes, stirring occasionally. Garnish the sauce with red basil leaves and serve with grated Parmesan.

10
PREP

30
COOK

4
SERVES

thick

4 tablespoons **olive oil**

2 **onions**, diced

2 **garlic cloves**, finely chopped

8 **anchovy fillets**, coarsely chopped

400 g (13 oz) can **plum tomatoes**, drained and diced

12 **black olives**, pitted and halved

1 tablespoon **capers**, drained

2 tablespoons chopped **oregano**

salt and **pepper**

red basil leaves, to garnish

125 g (4 oz) **Parmesan cheese**, freshly grated, to serve

500 g (1 lb) **aubergines**, roughly chopped

300 g (10 oz) **courgettes**, roughly chopped

3 **red peppers**, cored, deseeded and cut into chunks

2 **red onions**, chopped

2 teaspoons chopped **rosemary**

125 ml (4 fl oz) **olive oil**

1 tablespoon **balsamic vinegar**

1 tablespoon **clear honey**

salt and **pepper**

freshly grated **Parmesan cheese**, to serve

10

PREP

60

COOK

4

SERVES

tasty

Roasted vegetable sauce

The vegetables in this sauce are chopped up before being roasted, so they cook to an appetizing crispness. This sauce is perfect with a fresh ribbon pasta such as tagliatelle or pappardelle and goes well with a small sprinkling of a contrastingly salty cheese such as Parmesan, pecorino or grana padano.

1 Whiz the aubergines in a food processor until chopped into small, uneven pieces and tip into a large roasting tin. Whiz the courgettes and peppers and add to the tin. Stir in the onions and rosemary and drizzle with 100 ml (3½ fl oz) of the oil.

2 Roast the vegetables in a preheated oven, 200°C (400°F), Gas Mark 6, for about 1 hour, turning them frequently until they are deep golden and beginning to caramelize.

3 Blend the remaining oil with the balsamic vinegar and honey. Drizzle this over the vegetables, season lightly and mix well. Serve with grated Parmesan.

Three-cheese sauce

5

PREP

5

COOK

When mixing several cheeses in a dish it's best to use ones with strongly contrasting flavours and textures, such as provolone or fontina, ricotta, and Parmesan or pecorino.

1 Put the oil, chives, rosemary and cayenne pepper in a saucepan and heat gently for a couple of minutes so that the herbs and spice infuse the oil.

2 Stir in the ricotta and heat gently, stirring, until it has softened.

3 Stir in the remaining cheeses and heat through gently for 1 minute until the sauce is smooth and creamy.

2

SERVES

cheesy

4 tablespoons **lemon-infused olive oil**

3 tablespoons chopped **chives**

1 teaspoon finely chopped **rosemary**

good pinch of **cayenne pepper**

150 g (5 oz) **ricotta cheese**

50 g (2 oz) **provolone cheese** or **fontina cheese**, thinly sliced

50 g (2 oz) **Parmesan cheese** or **pecorino cheese**, freshly grated

1 kg (2 lb) fresh ripe **plum tomatoes**, quartered, or 2½ x 400 g (13 oz) cans plum tomatoes, drained and roughly chopped

1 **onion**, finely chopped

2 **garlic cloves**, chopped

4 **basil leaves**, bruised

125 ml (4 fl oz) **olive oil**

Basic tomato sauce

PREP

COOK

This is the perfect sauce for covering pizza bases, dressing pasta and enriching other sauces. Any sauce that you do not use straight away can be kept, covered, in the fridge for up to 1 week.

SERVES

simple

1 Place the tomatoes in a large saucepan with the onion and garlic. Cover the pan, bring to the boil, then cook slowly for 25 minutes.

2 Uncover the pan and simmer for another 15–30 minutes to evaporate any extra liquid, as the sauce should be quite thick.

3 Purée the sauce in a blender, then sieve it to remove any seeds and skin. Stir in the basil and oil.

Rich tomato sauce

For the true flavour of this sauce to develop, it is best to use those red plum tomatoes that have ripened slowly in the sun. When cooked with a pinch of sugar, they add a depth of sweetness to the overall flavour.

1 Heat the oil in a large saucepan. Add the onion, garlic, mushrooms and carrots, and fry over a moderate heat for 5 minutes or until softened.

2 Add the tomatoes, tomato purée and sugar and stir well. Bring to the boil, then reduce the heat, cover the pan and simmer for 20 minutes, stirring occasionally. Season to taste with salt and pepper.

3 Stir the cream into the sauce, garnish with oregano and serve with grated Parmesan.

20

PREP

30

COOK

4

SERVES

sweet

1 tablespoon **olive oil**

1 **onion**, chopped finely

2 **garlic cloves**, crushed

125 g (4 oz) **button mushrooms**, chopped finely

2 **carrots**, chopped finely

750 g (1½ lb) ripe **plum tomatoes**, skinned (see page 16) and chopped

2 tablespoons **tomato purée**

¼ teaspoon **caster sugar**

4 tablespoons **single cream**

salt and **pepper**

1 tablespoon **oregano leaves**, to garnish

freshly grated **Parmesan cheese**, to serve

2 **garlic cloves**, crushed

2 x 400 g (13 oz) cans **chopped tomatoes**

4 tablespoons **olive oil**

1 teaspoon **dried oregano**

1 teaspoon **caster sugar**

8 rashers of **smoked back bacon**, finely chopped

75 g (3 oz) **mascarpone cheese** or 75 ml (3 fl oz) **crème fraîche**

salt and **pepper**

5

PREP

15

COOK

4

SERVES

simple

Creamy tomato and bacon sauce

This is a good basic pasta sauce and can be made without the bacon for vegetarians. Make several batches, minus the mascarpone or crème fraîche, and freeze for future use.

1 Put the garlic, tomatoes, oil, oregano and sugar in a saucepan, bring to the boil, reduce the heat, cover and simmer for 10 minutes.

2 Add the bacon and simmer, uncovered, for a further 5 minutes. Season to taste with salt and pepper.

3 Stir in the mascarpone or crème fraîche, heat through, then taste the sauce and adjust the seasoning if necessary.

Chilli sauce

15

PREP

Pasta with chilli sauce is a true Italian classic. This recipe is not too hot, and once you've got used to the intense flavour of the chillies, you'll really enjoy it. For a milder flavour, remove the seeds.

45

COOK

1 Heat the oil in a pan and cook the onion, garlic and bacon until lightly coloured.

2 Add the chillies, tomatoes and 25 g (1 oz) of the cheese. Cook over a gentle heat for 30–40 minutes until the sauce thickens. Season to taste with salt and pepper.

4

SERVES

3 Serve at once sprinkled with pecorino or Parmesan shavings.

hot

1–2 tablespoons **olive oil**

1 large **onion**, finely chopped

2 **garlic cloves**, crushed

125 g (4 oz) rindless **streaky bacon**, chopped

1–2 fresh **red chillies** or **green chillies**, chopped

400 g (13 oz) can **chopped tomatoes**

50–75 g (2–3 oz) **pecorino cheese** or **Parmesan cheese**, shaved

salt and **pepper**

2 teaspoons **cardamom pods**

1 teaspoon **cumin seeds**

1 teaspoon **fennel seeds**

2 tablespoons **olive oil**

1 **red onion**, thinly sliced

500 g (1 lb) **sausages**, skins removed

50 g (2 oz) **pine nuts**

3 tablespoons chopped **herbs**, such as parsley, fennel and fresh coriander

150 g (5 oz) **green cabbage**, very finely shredded

300 ml (½ pint) **single cream**

salt and **pepper**

10
PREP

20
COOK

4

SERVES

spicy

Spicy sausage sauce

Packed with plenty of spices, this comforting sauce transforms even the dullest sausages into a deliciously meaty pasta topping. If possible, use sausages flavoured with apple, leek or mild spices.

1 Crush the cardamom pods using a pestle and mortar to release the seeds. Discard the shells and add the cumin and fennel seeds. Crush until lightly ground.

2 Heat the oil in a large, heavy-based frying pan and fry the onion for 3 minutes. Add the skinned sausages and fry gently, breaking them up into small pieces with a wooden spoon, for 6–8 minutes until cooked through.

3 Add the pine nuts and the crushed seeds to the pan and cook gently for 3–5 minutes, stirring frequently. Add the herbs and cabbage and fry for 2 minutes.

4 Pour in the cream and heat through for a further 2 minutes. Season to taste with salt and pepper.

Calabrian sauce

15
PREP

35
COOK

In Calabria this dish is served with grated ricotta that has been left to mature and is no longer a fresh curd cheese. Pecorino makes a perfectly acceptable replacement.

1 Crush the tomatoes or purée them briefly in a food processor.

2 Heat the oil in a heavy-based saucepan, add the garlic and chilli and fry gently until the garlic is golden, crushing the chilli against the bottom of the pan to release its flavour.

3 Add the tomatoes and the slices of salami and season to taste with salt. Bring to the boil, then reduce the heat and simmer gently for about 30 minutes, until the sauce becomes denser and darker in colour. Serve sprinkled with pecorino shavings.

4
SERVES

spicy

1½ x 400 g (13 oz) cans **plum tomatoes**

½ tablespoon **olive oil**

2 **garlic cloves**, each cut into 3–4 pieces

1 **chilli**, cored and deseeded

125 g (4 oz) **salami**, thickly sliced

salt

75 g (3 oz) **pecorino cheese**, shaved, to serve

meat

3 tablespoons **olive oil**

75 g (3 oz) **smoked bacon**, rind removed and diced

1 **onion**, finely chopped

5 **sage leaves**, plus extra to garnish (optional)

250 g (8 oz) can **borlotti beans**, rinsed and drained

2 tablespoons **chicken stock** (see page 19)

¼ teaspoon **plain flour**

1 tablespoon **tomato purée**

2 tablespoons **red wine**

salt and **pepper**

TO SERVE:

2 tablespoons freshly grated **Parmesan cheese**

1 tablespoon freshly grated **pecorino cheese**

10

PREP

10

COOK

4

SERVES

herby

Bacon, borlotti and sage sauce

Sage is widely used in Italian cooking, and it imparts a distinctive, pungent flavour. It combines very well with the beans, tomatoes, garlic and olive oil in this recipe.

1 Heat the oil in a large, heavy-based saucepan, add the bacon, onion and sage leaves and cook over a medium heat until golden. Add the borlotti beans.

2 Heat the stock. Mix the flour and tomato purée in a small bowl, then stir in the hot stock and the wine. Pour into the bean mixture, stirring with a wooden spoon, then cook over a low heat until the sauce thickens.

3 Remove the sage leaves and add salt and pepper to taste. Garnish with a few fresh sage leaves, if liked, and serve with grated Parmesan and pecorino.

Rich bolognese sauce

What could be more traditional than spaghetti Bolognese, with its rich, meaty sauce and piles of freshly cooked spaghetti? In fact, however, in Italy this is traditionally served with tagliatelle, not spaghetti.

20

PREP

120

COOK

4

SERVES

classic

3 tablespoons **olive oil**

25 g (1 oz) **butter**

½ small **onion**, finely chopped

12 small **carrot**, finely chopped

1 small **celery stick**, diced

25 g (1 oz) **mushrooms**, diced

1 **garlic clove**, finely chopped

50 g (2 oz) **ham** or lean **bacon**, diced

375 g (12 oz) lean minced **beef**

125 ml (4 fl oz) dry **red wine**

2 tablespoons finely chopped **parsley**, plus extra to garnish

2 teaspoons **plain flour**

300 ml (½ pint) **beef stock** (see page 20)

4 tablespoons **tomato purée**

150 ml (¼ pint) **double cream**

salt and **pepper**

freshly grated **Parmesan cheese**, to serve

1 Heat the oil and butter in a large saucepan and add the onion, carrot, celery, mushrooms and garlic. Gently fry until lightly browned. Add the ham and beef and fry a little longer until the beef is browned.

2 Stir in the wine and parsley, bring to the boil, then reduce the heat and simmer until the wine has reduced a little. Blend the flour with a little of the stock, add it to the mixture and stir until it thickens, then simmer gently for 10–15 minutes, stirring frequently.

3 Add the tomato purée and a little more stock. Simmer gently, covered, for 1½ hours, gradually stirring in the remaining stock, then season to taste with salt and pepper.

4 Stir in the cream and simmer, uncovered, until reduced. Garnish with the extra parsley and serve with grated Parmesan.

1 tablespoon **olive oil**

2 **spring onions**, chopped finely

2 tablespoons chopped **parsley**

2 tablespoons chopped **basil**

2 tablespoons chopped **thyme**, plus 1 tablespoon to garnish

2 tablespoons chopped **coriander**, plus 1 tablespoon to garnish

4 slices **prosciutto**, chopped

300 ml (½ pint) **double cream** or **crème fraîche**

salt and **pepper**

PREP 10

COOK 3

SERVES 4

quick

Four-herb and prosciutto sauce

Prosciutto is a highly regarded, flavoursome air-dried Italian ham, which is usually served in very thin slices. The best-known prosciutto comes from Parma and is also known as Parma ham.

1 Heat the olive oil in a saucepan. Add the spring onions and fry for 1 minute.

2 Stir in the herbs, prosciutto and cream. Bring to the boil, reduce the heat and simmer for 3 minutes, then season to taste with salt and pepper. Garnish with coriander and thyme mixed together.

Spicy tomato and pepperoni sauce

While this sauce simmers, the pungent, smoky flavour of the pepperoni transforms a fairly plain tomato sauce into something rather more special.

10

PREP

15

COOK

4

SERVES

spicy

1 Heat the oil in a large frying pan and add the garlic, chilli powder and coriander. Fry over a moderate heat for about 1 minute, stirring constantly.

2 Stir in the pepperoni, the tomatoes with their juices, passata and red wine. Bring to the boil, then reduce the heat and simmer, uncovered, for about 10 minutes. Season to taste with salt and pepper, then stir in the basil and sprinkle with thyme.

2 tablespoons **olive oil**

3 **garlic cloves**, crushed

1 teaspoon mild **chilli powder**

1 teaspoon **ground coriander**

125 g (4 oz) **pepperoni**, sliced

400 g (13 oz) can **chopped tomatoes**

6 tablespoons **passata** (sieved tomatoes)

4 tablespoons **red wine**

1 tablespoon **basil leaves**

salt and **pepper**

sprigs of **thyme**, to garnish

75 ml (3 fl oz) **olive oil**

1 large **onion**, finely chopped

1 **garlic clove**, finely chopped

1 kg (2 lb) ripe **tomatoes**, skinned (see page 16) and roughly chopped

2 tablespoons chopped **oregano**

75 g (3 oz) **pancetta**, chopped

salt and **pepper**

15

PREP

25

COOK

4

SERVES

fresh

Tomato and pancetta sauce

A fresh tomato sauce is worth making only if you can get hold of really tasty, well-flavoured tomatoes. Even better is a glut of home-grown ones so you can make large quantities for the freezer.

1 Heat the oil in a large, heavy-based saucepan and add the onion and garlic. Fry over a gentle heat, stirring frequently, until the onion is soft. Add the tomatoes, oregano and a little salt and pepper.

2 Bring to a bubble, then reduce the heat and let the sauce cook gently, covered with a lid, for about 15 minutes until thickened and pulpy. Break up the tomatoes frequently during cooking.

3 Meanwhile, dry-fry the pancetta in a small pan until crisp. Add to the cooked sauce and check the seasoning.

Bacon, mushroom and tomato sauce

Slow-cooking the tomato sauce before adding the bacon and mushrooms ensures that these ingredients retain their identity rather than breaking down into the sauce.

15

PREP

35

COOK

4

SERVES

tasty

50 g (2 oz) **butter**

175 g (6 oz) lean **bacon**, diced

375 g (12 oz) **mushrooms**, sliced

2 **garlic cloves**, sliced

½ **chilli**

500 g (1 lb) **tomatoes**, skinned (see page 16) and chopped

handful of **basil leaves**, torn

salt

125 g (4 oz) **Parmesan cheese** or **pecorino cheese**, freshly grated, to serve

1 Melt the butter in a frying pan, add the bacon and fry gently until lightly browned. Remove from the pan with a slotted spoon and drain on kitchen paper.

2 Fry the mushrooms in the butter that is remaining in the pan. Remove with a slotted spoon, and set aside.

3 Fry the garlic and the chilli in the same frying pan. When the garlic is golden-brown, discard it together with the chilli.

4 Add the tomatoes to the pan with the basil. Bring to the boil, then reduce the heat and simmer for 20 minutes. Season to taste with salt.

5 Stir in the bacon and mushrooms and simmer gently for a few more minutes. Serve with grated Parmesan or pecorino.

4 tablespoons **olive oil**

1 **onion**, finely chopped

125 g (4 oz) **prosciutto**, diced

2 **garlic cloves**, crushed

1 **chilli**, deseeded and finely chopped

750 g (1½ lb) **tomatoes**, skinned (see page 16) and chopped

salt and **pepper**

75 g (3 oz) **pecorino cheese**, freshly grated, to serve

15

PREP

20

COOK

4–6

SERVES

spicy

Prosciutto, chilli and tomato sauce

This is a remarkably simple sauce but it still has lots of flavour from the smoky prosciutto and the hot chilli.

1 Heat the oil in a large saucepan and fry the onion for 3 minutes. Add the prosciutto and cook for a further 2–3 minutes.

2 Add the garlic, chilli and tomatoes, bring to the boil, then reduce the heat and simmer for 10 minutes until thickened. Season to taste with salt and pepper and serve with grated pecorino.

Bacon and broad bean sauce

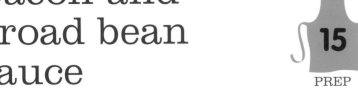

The bright green broad beans are quite eye-catching in this creamy sauce, which has streaky bacon for added flavour.

15

PREP

15

COOK

4

SERVES

filling

375 g (12 oz) small shelled **broad beans**

25 g (1 oz) **butter**

2 **shallots**, finely chopped

250 g (8 oz) **unsmoked streaky bacon**, rind removed and diced

2 teaspoons chopped **thyme**

grated **rind of ½ lemon**

300 ml (½ pint) **whipping cream**

pepper

3 tablespoons chopped **flat leaf parsley**, to garnish

freshly grated **Parmesan cheese**, to serve

1 Plunge the broad beans into boiling water for 2 minutes. Remove and drain under cold running water, then slip off the outer skins if they are tough.

2 Melt the butter in a large saucepan and gently fry the shallots and bacon for 4–5 minutes. Stir in the thyme, lemon rind, cream and pepper to taste.

3 Bring the sauce to the boil, then reduce the heat and simmer for 5 minutes. Stir in the broad beans. Garnish with parsley and serve with grated Parmesan.

5 tablespoons **olive oil**

3 large **onions**, thinly sliced into rings

250 g (8 oz) **pepperoni**, sliced

300 ml (½ pint) **stock** of choice (see pages 18–21)

4 tablespoons chopped **flat leaf parsley**

1 tablespoon **balsamic vinegar**

salt and **pepper**

10
PREP

50
COOK

4–6
SERVES

sweet

Peperoni, onion and balsamic sauce

Caramelizing the onions gives this sauce an essential sweetness, which is then cut through by the balsamic vinegar, to give a perfect balance of flavours.

1 Heat the oil in a large saucepan and fry the onions over a low heat for 40 minutes, until very soft and slightly caramelised.

2 Raise the heat, add the pepperoni and stir-fry for a few minutes until heated through.

3 Pour in the stock and bring to the boil, scraping up any sediment from the bottom of the pan. Stir in the parsley and vinegar and season to taste with salt and pepper.

Broad bean, prosciutto and mint sauce

This recipe is a good example of how many Italian pasta recipes use olive oil more as a dressing than a sauce, so that it delicately coats the pasta.

1 Bring a pan of salted water to the boil and cook the broad beans for 2–3 minutes.

2 Drain the beans quickly and toss them in the oil with the lemon rind, prosciutto, spring onions and mint leaves. Serve scattered with the mozzarella.

8

PREP

3

COOK

4

SERVES

stylish

250 g (8 oz) shelled baby **broad beans**

4–6 tablespoons extra virgin **olive oil**

grated **rind of 1 lemon**

175 g (6 oz) **prosciutto**, shredded

3–4 **spring onions**, finely sliced

8–10 **mint leaves**, shredded

salt

125 g (4 oz) **buffalo mozzarella cheese**, diced, to serve

2 tablespoons **olive oil**

1 **garlic clove**, crushed and chopped

250 g (8 oz) **porcini**, sliced

250 g (8 oz) **prosciutto**, cut into strips

150 ml (¼ pint) **whipping cream**

handful of **flat leaf parsley**, chopped

salt and **pepper**

75 g (3 oz) **Parmesan cheese**, freshly grated, to serve

10
PREP

8
COOK

4
SERVES

quick

Prosciutto and porcini sauce

Fresh or dried porcini may be used for this recipe. If you decide to use dried porcini, use 125 g (4 oz) and soak them in hot water for 15 minutes to rehydrate them first.

1 Heat the olive oil in a saucepan, add the garlic and porcini and sauté for 4 minutes over a moderate heat.

2 Add the prosciutto, cream and parsley and season with salt and pepper. Bring to the boil, then reduce the heat and simmer for 1 minute. Serve with grated Parmesan.

Jerusalem artichoke and bacon sauce

The flavour of these artichokes vaguely resembles that of globe artichoke hearts, and they make an equally good partner to pasta.

15

PREP

25

COOK

4

SERVES

rustic

1 Cook the artichokes in boiling water for 8–10 minutes until they are just tender. Peel, if necessary, and cut into thin slices.

2 Melt half the butter in a saucepan and fry the bacon until it is beginning to colour. Add the onion, celery and cayenne pepper and fry for a further 5 minutes.

3 Stir in the stock and the artichokes and bring to the boil. Cover, reduce the heat and simmer gently for 5 minutes. Stir in the cream and chives and season to taste with salt and pepper.

400 g (13 oz) **Jerusalem artichokes**, peeled if fairly smooth, otherwise skins left on

25 g (1 oz) **butter**

150 g (5 oz) **streaky bacon**, chopped

1 **onion**, finely chopped

1 **celery stick**, chopped

¼ teaspoon **cayenne pepper**

150 ml (¼ pint) **chicken stock** or **vegetable stock** (see pages 19 and 21)

3 tablespoons **double cream**

3 tablespoons chopped **chives**

salt and **pepper**

1 kg (2 lb) **butternut squash**, peeled and cut into 2.5 cm (1 inch) chunks

4–5 **garlic cloves**

4 tablespoons **olive oil**

½ teaspoon crushed **chilli flakes**

2 tablespoons **pine nuts**

150 g (5 oz) piece of **smoked bacon**, diced

50 g (2 oz) **mixed, stuffed, spicy-marinated olives**, roughly chopped

1 **roasted pepper**, cut into strips (optional)

200 ml (7 fl oz) **crème fraîche**

salt and **pepper**

deep-fried **sage leaves**, to garnish

freshly grated **Parmesan cheese**, to serve

12

PREP

45

COOK

4

SERVES

spicy

Squash, bacon and olive sauce

Combine these easily prepared ingredients with penne pasta and you have the perfect comfort dish for winter! The garlic-infused squash will add a sweet taste to the sauce.

1 Toss the butternut squash and the garlic cloves in 3 tablespoons of the olive oil, add the chilli flakes and season with salt and pepper. Tip into a large roasting tin and bake in a preheated oven, 190°C (375°F), Gas Mark 5, for about 45 minutes until the squash is soft and golden.

2 Meanwhile, heat the remaining oil in a frying pan and fry the pine nuts over a low heat, moving them quickly around the pan, until they are golden-brown. Drain on kitchen paper. Add the bacon and fry gently until it is golden and crispy. Add the olives and pepper, if using, and warm through for 2–3 minutes.

3 When the squash is cooked, toss it with the pine nuts, bacon, olives and roasted pepper, if using, and stir in the crème fraîche. Garnish with deep-fried sage leaves and serve with grated Parmesan.

Bacon, garlic and fennel sauce

With its liquorice-like taste, fennel is a great way to make an impact. Combined here with bacon, garlic and fromage frais, it makes a great-tasting sauce.

15

PREP

12

COOK

4–6

SERVES

tasty

6 rashers of **unsmoked streaky bacon**, rind removed

2 tablespoons **olive oil**

2 **fennel bulbs**, finely chopped

2 **garlic cloves**, finely chopped

4 tablespoons freshly grated **Parmesan cheese**

300 ml (½ pint) **fromage frais**

3 tablespoons finely chopped **parsley**

fennel fronds, to garnish

1 Grill the bacon until it is crisp. Drain on kitchen paper and set aside.

2 Heat the oil in a frying pan, add the fennel and garlic, cover with a lid and cook gently over a low heat for 5 minutes until the fennel is just tender.

3 Add the Parmesan, fromage frais and parsley to the pan, and season to taste with salt and pepper. Bring to the boil, then reduce the heat and simmer over a low heat for 1–2 minutes.

4 Chop the bacon and sprinkle it over the sauce, then garnish with fennel fronds.

50 g (2 oz) **butter**

250 g (8 oz) **pancetta**, diced

1 **carrot**, diced

4 **celery sticks**, diced

1 **garlic clove**, finely chopped

3 tablespoons **tomato purée**

250 ml (8 fl oz) **chicken stock** (see page 19)

salt and **pepper**

freshly grated **Parmesan cheese**, to serve

15
PREP

20
COOK

Pancetta and celery sauce

Celery adds a subtle flavour to any dish it features in, and here it teams up wonderfully with the pancetta to make a memorable sauce.

4
SERVES

subtle

1 Melt the butter in a saucepan. Add the pancetta, carrot, celery and garlic, and fry gently for 5 minutes.

2 Stir in the tomato purée and stock, bring to the boil and simmer for 15 minutes. Season to taste with salt and pepper, then serve with grated Parmesan.

Pancetta, bean and garlic sauce

Flageolet beans are tiny pulses that can be used to add flavour and protein to dishes without dominating them. Combined with pancetta or bacon, they make this creamy sauce a winner.

1 Heat the oil in a frying pan and fry the pancetta until it is lightly browned. Add the garlic and chilli flakes and fry until the garlic is just pale golden.

2 Gently stir in the beans and cream. Bring to the boil, then reduce the heat and simmer for a few minutes until heated through. Season to taste with salt and pepper and garnish with coriander.

5

PREP

8

COOK

4

SERVES

hearty

2 tablespoons **olive oil**

275 g (9 oz) **pancetta** or **smoked streaky bacon**, rind removed and diced

2 **garlic cloves**, finely chopped

½ teaspoon **dried chilli flakes**

400 g (13 oz) can **flageolet beans**, drained and rinsed

300 ml (½ pint) **whipping cream**

salt and **pepper**

2 tablespoons chopped fresh **coriander**, to garnish

3 tablespoons **olive oil**

2 **shallots**, finely chopped

8 slices of **unsmoked pancetta**, chopped

2 teaspoons crushed **dried chilli flakes**

1¼ x 400 g (13 oz) cans **chopped tomatoes**

salt and **pepper**

sprigs of **parsley**, to garnish

MOLLICA:

6 slices of **white bread**, crusts removed

125 g (4 oz) **butter**

2 **garlic cloves**, finely chopped

5

PREP

30

COOK

4

SERVES

spicy

Arrabiata sauce with garlic crumbs

This is a hot and spicy sauce, which has the added crunch of golden fried breadcrumbs, called *mollica* in Sicilian or, more accurately, *mollica fritta*. You can even just toss plain pasta in the crumbs for a simple meal.

1 Heat the oil in a saucepan and gently fry the shallots and pancetta gently for 6–8 minutes until they are golden. Add the chilli flakes and chopped tomatoes, bring to the boil, then half-cover the pan, reduce the heat and simmer for 20 minutes until the sauce is thick and has reduced. Season to taste with salt and pepper.

2 Meanwhile, make the mollica. Put the bread into a food processor and reduce to crumbs. Heat the butter in a frying pan, add the garlic and breadcrumbs and stir-fry until golden and crisp. (Don't let the crumbs catch and burn or the dish will be ruined.)

3 Scatter the tomato sauce with the garlic crumbs and garnish with parsley.

Sausage, cream and mustard sauce

When you need some real comfort food, go for this satisfying pasta dish. It's hearty and sustaining and makes a great winter supper or leisurely weekend lunch. Choose good-quality sausages with loads of herbs and a high meat content.

1 Heat the oil in a frying pan and fry the sausage meat for 3 minutes until it is lightly golden, breaking it up with a wooden spoon. Add the garlic and fry for another 1 minute.

2 Pour in the wine and let it bubble up, scraping any sediment off the bottom of the frying pan. Simmer for 3 minutes until the wine has nearly evaporated, then stir in the mustard and crème fraîche.

3 Season the sauce with nutmeg and salt and pepper, garnish with herbs and serve with grated Parmesan.

10

PREP

10

COOK

4

SERVES

hearty

1 tablespoon **olive oil**

500 g (1 lb) **herby pork sausages**, skinned

2 **garlic cloves**, sliced

150 ml (¼ pint) **white wine**

1 tablespoon **wholegrain mustard**

200 g (7 oz) **crème fraîche**

pinch of grated **nutmeg**

salt and **pepper**

handful of **oregano leaves** or chopped **flat leaf parsley**, to garnish

freshly grated **Parmesan cheese**, to serve

25 g (1 oz) **butter**

400 g (13 oz) **game sausages**, skinned

1 large **onion**, finely chopped

1 teaspoon chopped **rosemary**

200 ml (7 fl oz) **red wine**

200 g (7 oz) cooked **chestnuts**, chopped

4 **pickled walnuts**, chopped, plus 3 tablespoons vinegar from the jar

4 tablespoons chopped **flat leaf parsley**

salt and **pepper**

15

PREP

25

COOK

4

SERVES

feast

Sausage, chestnut and walnut sauce

Venison, wild boar or any of the other gamey sausages are ideal for this dish, which makes a comforting and warming winter supper served over pasta.

1 Melt the butter in a large saucepan. Add the skinned sausages, one at a time, mashing them in the pan with a fork to break them into small pieces.

2 Add the onion and fry gently, stirring and continuing to break up the sausages with the edge of a wooden spoon, for about 10 minutes or until browned.

3 Stir in the rosemary and wine and cook gently for 5 minutes.

4 Add the chestnuts, walnuts and the vinegar from the jar. Heat gently for 5 minutes until warmed through. Stir in the parsley and season to taste with salt and pepper.

Sausage and tomato sauce

15
PREP

25
COOK

4
SERVES

rustic

This rustic, warming sauce is perfect winter food: tasty, filling and comforting. Served with a steaming bowl of freshly cooked pasta, it will gladden the heart and taste buds alike.

1 Heat the oil in a large saucepan and gently fry the onion until soft. Add the garlic and fry until beginning to colour.

2 Add the sausage to the pan and fry until evenly browned, then add the remaining ingredients and cook gently, uncovered, for about 12–15 minutes. Season to taste with salt and pepper.

1 tablespoon **olive oil**

1 large **onion**, chopped

2 **garlic cloves**, crushed

500 g (1 lb) **Italian sausage**, skinned and roughly chopped

1 **red pepper**, cored, deseeded and cut into 1 cm (½ inch) squares

750 g (1½ lb) **tomatoes**, skinned (see page 16) and chopped

2 teaspoons **dried oregano**

2 tablespoons **tomato purée**

salt and **pepper**

25 g (1 oz) **butter**

250 g (8 oz) **Italian sausages**, skinned and crumbled

125 g (4 oz) **mascarpone cheese**

2 **egg yolks**

1 **egg white**

25 g (1 oz) **Parmesan cheese**, freshly grated

¼ teaspoon grated **nutmeg**

salt

15

PREP

5

COOK

4

SERVES

rich

Sausage and mascarpone sauce

This unusual recipe is a bit like the pasta sauce version of a cooked breakfast. Serve with penne or other robust, shaped pasta.

1 Melt the butter in a frying pan, add the crumbled sausages and cook over a low heat for 5 minutes until lightly browned.

2 Mix the mascarpone cheese with the egg yolks and white, beating hard with a wooden spoon. When soft, add the Parmesan cheese, nutmeg and a pinch of salt.

3 Mix the sausage and cooking juices with the cheese mixture.

Aubergine, tomato and bacon sauce

Cooking the aubergine separately, rather than within the sauce, means that it is still golden and slightly crispy when it is stirred into the sauce.

50
PREP

35
COOK

4
SERVES

simple

1 large **aubergine**, diced

125–150 ml (4–5 fl oz) **olive oil**, plus 1 tablespoon

1 **onion**, chopped

2 **garlic cloves**, crushed

2 rashers of **streaky bacon**, rind removed and chopped

400 g (13 oz) can **chopped tomatoes**

salt and **pepper**

basil sprigs and leaves, to garnish

1 Put the diced aubergine in a colander and sprinkle with salt. Leave for at least 30 minutes to drain, which will remove some of the bitter aubergine juices. Rinse thoroughly, drain well and dry on kitchen paper.

2 Heat the 1 tablespoon of oil in a frying pan, add the onion, garlic and bacon and fry gently until soft. Add the tomatoes, season, bring to the boil, then reduce the heat and simmer for 25–30 minutes until the sauce is thickened. (For a smoother sauce, liquidize, then sieve to remove the seeds.)

3 Meanwhile, heat half the remaining oil in a frying pan and cook some of the aubergine dice until golden-brown. Repeat, adding more oil to the pan if necessary, until all of the aubergine is well cooked.

4 Stir the aubergine into the tomato sauce and garnish with basil.

50 g (2 oz) **butter**

250 g (8 oz) **mushrooms**, thinly sliced

100 g (4 oz) frozen **peas**

300 ml (½ pint) **single cream**

125 g (4 oz) lean cooked **ham**, cut into matchstick strips

125 g (4 oz) **Parmesan cheese**, freshly grated

salt and **pepper**

10

PREP

15

COOK

Ham, pea and mushroom sauce

If peas are in season, buy them fresh and pod them yourself. Although the flavour of frozen peas is extremely comparable to fresh, there's nothing quite like preparing them yourself.

4

SERVES

fresh

1 Melt half the butter and gently fry the mushrooms until just tender. Season to taste.

2 Meanwhile, cook the peas in boiling salted water until tender, then drain.

3 Put the remaining butter and the cream into a saucepan and heat gently without allowing the mixture to boil. Add the mushrooms with their juice, the peas and the ham. Add one-third of the grated Parmesan and heat. Serve with the remaining cheese.

Bacon and fennel sauce

This is a simple combination that uses bold flavours to make it stand out from the crowd. The contrast of the creamy sauce with the crispy bacon is a taste sensation.

10

PREP

10

COOK

4

SERVES

simple

6 rashers **unsmoked streaky bacon**, rind removed

2 tablespoons **olive oil**

2 **fennel bulbs**, chopped

2 **garlic cloves**, finely chopped

4 tablespoons freshly grated **Parmesan cheese**

300 ml (½ pint) **fromage frais**

3 tablespoons finely chopped **parsley**

salt and **pepper**

fennel fronds, to garnish

1 Grill the bacon until it is crisp. Drain on kitchen paper, chop and set aside.

2 Heat the oil in a saucepan and add the fennel and garlic. Cover with a lid and cook over a low heat for 5 minutes until the fennel is just tender.

3 Add the Parmesan, fromage frais and parsley, and season to taste with salt and peper. Bring to the boil, then reduce the heat and simmer over a low heat for 1–2 minutes. Garnish with fennel fronds and sprinkle with chopped bacon.

3 **chicken legs**

3 **carrots**, roughly chopped

1 large **onion**, roughly chopped

2 **celery sticks**, roughly chopped

2 **bay leaves**

200 ml (7 fl oz) **crème fraîche**

3 tablespoons roughly chopped **tarragon**

salt and **pepper**

10

PREP

70

COOK

4

SERVES

meaty

Chicken and tarragon sauce

Although this sauce is thin in consistency, it's packed with meaty flavour. Toss the sauce with fusilli pasta, which will trap all the delicious juices.

1 Halve the chicken legs through the joints to separate the thighs from the drumsticks and put them in a large saucepan. Scatter the carrots, onion, celery and bay leaves on top and just cover with water. Heat until simmering, then reduce the heat to its lowest setting and cook very gently, uncovered, for about 50 minutes or until the chicken pieces are very tender.

2 Lift out the chicken. Strain the stock, discarding the vegetables and bay leaves, and return to the pan. Bring the stock to the boil and boil rapidly until it is reduced to about a ladleful. This will take 15–20 minutes.

3 Once the chicken is cool enough to handle, chop it into small pieces, discarding the skin and bones.

4 Stir the chicken, crème fraîche, tarragon and a little salt and pepper into the reduced stock and heat through gently before serving.

Chicken and rosemary sauce

Chicken and rosemary make a classic flavour combination. Rosemary is used in a number of pasta sauces, and it is really easy to grow yourself, even if you have little space – a simple windowbox will do.

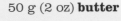

15

PREP

30

COOK

4

SERVES

classic

50 g (2 oz) **butter**

1 small **onion**, finely chopped

250 g (8 oz) white **button mushrooms**, thinly sliced

2 **garlic cloves**, crushed

1½ tablespoons **plain flour**

250 ml (8 fl oz) **chicken stock** (see page 19)

500–750 g (1–1½ lb) boneless, skinless **chicken breasts**, diagonally cut into thin strips

4 tablespoons **medium dry sherry**

2 teaspoons chopped **rosemary**, plus extra to garnish

150 ml (¼ pint) **double cream**

salt and **pepper**

1 Melt the butter in a large saucepan. Add the onion and cook gently, stirring, for about 5 minutes. Add the mushrooms and garlic and stir over a moderate heat until the juices run. Remove the mushrooms and set aside.

2 Add the flour to the juices and cook gently, stirring, for 1 minute.

3 Gradually blend in the stock and bring the mixture to the boil, stirring. Reduce the heat and simmer for 3 minutes. Add the chicken, sherry and rosemary and season to taste with salt and pepper. Cover and simmer for 15 minutes, stirring occasionally.

4 Remove the sauce from the heat and stir in the cream and mushrooms. Return to the lowest heat for 1–2 minutes, stirring, then garnish with rosemary.

3 part-boned **chicken breasts**

1 small **onion**, quartered

1 **carrot**, chopped roughly

1 **bouquet garni**

a few **black peppercorns**

300 ml (½ pint) **water**

2 tablespoons **dry sherry** (optional)

50 g (2 oz) **butter**

250 g (8 oz) white **button mushrooms**, sliced thinly

2 **garlic cloves**, crushed

1 teaspoon chopped **rosemary**, plus extra to garnish

1½ tablespoons **plain flour**

150 ml (¼ pint) **double cream**

salt and **pepper**

30

PREP

25

COOK

4

SERVES

stylish

Chicken and mushroom sauce

Although this recipe has a number of steps, it is well worth the effort. It is important to allow the chicken to poach gently with the other ingredients because this will impart a distinctive flavour to the finished dish.

1 Put the chicken in a saucepan with the onion, carrot, bouquet garni and peppercorns. Pour in the water and sherry, if using. Boil, then lower the heat, cover and poach the chicken for 20 minutes until just tender.

2 Meanwhile, melt the butter in a separate saucepan, then add the mushrooms, garlic, rosemary and season to taste, and sauté over a moderate heat, for about 5 minutes until the juices run. Remove from the heat. With a slotted spoon, transfer the mushrooms from the buttery liquid to a bowl.

3 Lift the chicken from the saucepan, then strain the liquid into a jug. Cut the chicken into strips, discarding the skin and bones.

4 Return the mushroom liquid to the heat, sprinkle in the flour and then cook for 1–2 minutes, stirring. Add the chicken liquid, a little at a time, beating after each addition.

5 Boil, stirring. Lower the heat and add the chicken, mushrooms, cream and seasoning. Simmer, stirring frequently, for 5 minutes until thickened. Garnish with rosemary.

Chicken and tomato sauce

PREP 5

Always use a decent wine when cooking – it's a false economy to pour in cheap plonk. A hearty Italian red would be perfect for this flavoursome sauce.

COOK 20

1 Heat the oil in a saucepan and fry the chicken, stirring occasionally, until lightly coloured. Add the onion, celery and carrots, and cook for 5 minutes until softened.

2 Add the oregano, wine and tomatoes, and season to taste with salt and pepper. Bring to the boil, cover, then reduce the heat and simmer for 10 minutes. Garnish with oregano and serve with Parmesan shavings.

SERVES 4–6

rich

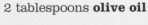

2 tablespoons **olive oil**

250 g (8 oz) boneless, skinless **chicken breasts**, diced

1 large **onion**, finely chopped

3 **celery sticks**, diced

2 **carrots**, diced

2 teaspoons **dried oregano**

125 ml (4 fl oz) **red wine**

400 g (13 oz) can **chopped tomatoes**

salt and **pepper**

1 tablespoon **oregano leaves**, to garnish

Parmesan cheese shavings, to serve

375 g (12 oz) **chicken livers**

2 tablespoons **olive oil**

½ **onion**, finely chopped

1 **garlic clove**, finely chopped

1 tablespoon finely chopped **parsley**

1 tablespoon finely chopped **marjoram**

175 g (6 oz) **mushrooms**, sliced

150 ml (¼ pint) **red wine**

150 ml (¼ pint) **chicken stock** (see page 19)

salt and **pepper**

Chicken liver sauce

15

PREP

25

COOK

4

SERVES

hearty

Chicken stock is one of the main ingredients in this recipe, so it would be best to use a good, homemade stock. This can be prepared in advance and kept in the freezer until needed. Serve this sauce with tagliatelle, lasagnette or pappardelle.

1 If using thawed frozen chicken livers, pat them dry on kitchen paper. Cut away any sinews and chop the livers into small pieces. Season with salt and pepper.

2 Heat the oil in a large saucepan and fry the onion and garlic for 5 minutes until soft. Add the liver, herbs and mushrooms and fry until the liver is lightly browned.

3 Add the wine and stock and season well. Bring to the boil, stirring, then reduce the heat, cover and simmer for 15 minutes.

Chicken liver, mushroom and Marsala sauce

Marsala wine and fruit vinegar give a sweet tang to this delicious sauce, balancing the richness of the chicken livers. Serve it with fresh spinach or mushroom tagliatelle for a light lunch or supper.

10
PREP

10
COOK

2
SERVES

sweet

1 If using thawed frozen chicken livers, pat them dry on kitchen paper. Cut away any sinews and chop the livers into small pieces. Season with salt and pepper.

2 Melt half the butter with the oil in a large, heavy-based frying pan. Add the livers and onion and fry quickly, stirring, for about 3 minutes until golden. Remove with a slotted spoon. Melt the remaining butter in the pan, add the mushrooms and garlic and cook, stirring, for 2 minutes.

3 Return the livers to the pan and add the Marsala, vinegar and seasoning. Cover and cook gently for 3–4 minutes until the livers are still slightly pink in the centre. Garnish with coriander.

250 g (8 oz) **chicken livers**

25 g (1 oz) **butter**

1 tablespoon **olive oil**

1 small **onion**, finely chopped

200 g (7 oz) **chestnut mushrooms**, finely chopped

2 **garlic cloves**, sliced

4 tablespoons **Marsala wine**

1 tablespoon **fruit vinegar**

salt and **pepper**

2 tablespoons chopped fresh **coriander leaves**, to garnish

200 g (7 oz) lean **pork**, roughly chopped

4 **pigeon breasts**, roughly chopped

8 **juniper berries**

25 g (1 oz) **butter**

1 **onion**, chopped

2 **garlic cloves**, crushed

2 **bay leaves**

several sprigs of **thyme**

250 g (8 oz) **mixed wild mushrooms**, such as girolles, chanterelles or ceps, sliced if large

150 ml (¼ pint) **chicken stock** (see page 19)

100 ml (3½ fl oz) **double cream**

2 tablespoons chopped **parsley**

salt and **pepper**

20

PREP

20

COOK

4

SERVES

meaty

Game and mushroom sauce

Pasta sauces range from delicate to intensely rich and meaty. This is definitely one of the latter: a wintry comfort food that combines delicious seasonal ingredients.

1 Blitz the pork in a food processor until chopped into very small pieces. Remove from the processor. Add the pigeon breasts to the processor and whiz until finely chopped.

2 Use a pestle and mortar to crush the juniper berries. Melt the butter in a large frying pan, add the pork, pigeon breasts and onion and fry gently, stirring frequently, until pale golden. Add the garlic, bay leaves, thyme and juniper and cook gently for a further 5 minutes.

3 Add the mushrooms and continue cooking for about 5 minutes or until the moisture from the mushrooms has evaporated.

4 Stir in the stock and cream and heat until the sauce is bubbling. Cook for about 3 minutes until heated through. Stir in the parsley and season to taste with salt and pepper.

Pâté and cream sauce

10
PREP

3
COOK

4
SERVES

posh

You can vary the flavour of this delicious sauce each time you make it according to the type of pâté that you choose. For a special occasion, perhaps you could use a can of pâté de foie gras. For those who prefer fish, use a smooth salmon pâté.

1 Put the pâté in a heavy saucepan with the garlic purée and the wine or water. Beat them well together. Gradually beat in all but 4 tablespoons of the cream until it is evenly incorporated. Stir in the mushrooms.

2 Place the saucepan over a gentle heat and stir until the sauce is heated through. Season to taste with salt and pepper, then garnish with rosemary

75 g (3 oz) fine, smooth **liver pâté**, at room temperature

1–2 teaspoons **garlic purée**, according to taste

4 tablespoons dry **white wine** or **water**

150 ml (¼ pint) **single cream**

300 g (10 oz) can whole **button mushrooms**, drained

salt and **pepper**

sprigs of **rosemary**, to garnish

500 g (1 lb) lean minced **lamb**

1 large **red onion**, finely chopped

2 tablespoons finely chopped **oregano**

50 g (2 oz) **breadcrumbs**

3 tablespoons **olive oil**

3 **garlic cloves**, crushed

500 g (1 lb) ripe **tomatoes**, skinned and chopped

1 teaspoon **caster sugar**

1 teaspoon **mild chilli powder**

finely grated **rind of 1 lemon**

salt and **pepper**

25

PREP

25

COOK

4

SERVES

spicy

Spicy meatball sauce

This recipe combines chunky, herby lamb meatballs and a tangy, fresh tomato sauce. Well-flavoured tomatoes are essential, but you can use canned tomatoes instead of fresh if the season dictates.

1 Put the lamb, onion, oregano, bread-crumbs and a little salt and pepper in a bowl and mix well together with your hands. Shape the mixture into small balls about 3 cm (1¼ inches) in diameter.

2 Heat the oil in a large frying pan and gently fry the meatballs, shaking the pan frequently, for 8–10 minutes or until they are browned on all sides.

3 Remove the meatballs from the frying pan with a slotted spoon and set aside. Then add the garlic, tomatoes, sugar, chilli powder and lemon rind to the pan. Heat gently, stirring, until the mixture is bubbling. Season to taste with salt and pepper.

4 Return the meatballs to the pan, cover with a lid and cook gently for 10 minutes or until they are cooked through and tender.

Lamb, leek and peppercorn sauce

Use good-quality lamb for this rich, creamy sauce so that it's not too watery when you fry it off. Serve with a plain or a spinach-flavoured pasta.

10
PREP

20
COOK

4
SERVES

meaty

1 Melt the butter in a large, shallow pan and gently fry the lamb until lightly browned, stirring frequently and breaking up the meat with a wooden spoon. Add the leeks and garlic and fry gently for a further 5 minutes.

2 Stir in the flour, then the stock and the peppercorns. Bring to the boil, then reduce the heat and simmer. Cover with a lid and cook gently for 10 minutes until the lamb is tender.

3 Stir in the crème fraîche, plenty of nutmeg and a little salt to taste. Heat through gently before serving.

25 g (1 oz) **butter**

400 g (13 oz) lean minced **lamb**

2 **leeks**, trimmed and chopped

2 **garlic cloves**, crushed

2 teaspoons **plain flour**

150 ml (¼ pint) **chicken stock** or **vegetable stock** (see pages 19 and 21)

2 tablespoons **green peppercorns in brine**, drained and rinsed

100 ml (3½ fl oz) **crème fraîche**

plenty of freshly grated **nutmeg**

salt

3 tablespoons **olive oil**

½ **onion**, finely chopped

1 **carrot**, finely diced

2 **celery sticks**, finely diced

2 **garlic cloves**, finely chopped

450 g (1 lb) **pork** fillet, cut into 1 cm (½ inch) cubes

2 teaspoons finely chopped **rosemary**

finely grated **rind of ¼ lemon**

400 g (13 oz) can **chopped tomatoes**

250 ml (8 fl oz) **chicken stock** (see page 19)

salt and **pepper**

2 tablespoons chopped **flat leaf parsley**, to garnish

50 g (2 oz) **Parmesan cheese**, freshly grated, to serve

20 PREP

40 COOK

4 SERVES

hearty

Pork and rosemary sauce

This is a chunky sauce that's perfect for cold winter evenings. The lemon rind adds a zingy contrast to the pork, while the parsley cuts through with a fresh, clean flavour. Serve with conchiglie pasta or gnocchi.

1 Heat the oil in a saucepan and gently fry the onion until golden. Add the carrot, celery and garlic and fry gently for about 5 minutes.

2 Stir in the pork, rosemary and lemon rind, and fry until the pork is lightly browned. Season to taste.

3 Add the tomatoes and stock. Bring to the boil, then simmer over a low heat for 30 minutes. Garnish with parsley and serve with grated Parmesan.

Hare sauce

This is a really rich, wintry sauce, redolent of Tuscany. Serve with pappardelle. To make a much lighter sauce, use a jointed rabbit instead of a hare and make it finer and smoother by liquidizing it.

1 Cut all the meat off the hare with a sharp knife, then cut it into small dice.

2 Heat the oil and butter in a frying pan and add the diced onion, carrot, celery and garlic. Stir well and cook gently for about 10 minutes until soft and beginning to brown.

3 Add the pancetta and hare, stir well and cook for a couple of minutes until the meat is browned. Stir in the flour, then the wine and half of the stock. Mix well, scraping up any sediment from the bottom of the pan.

4 Add the rosemary, sage and bay leaves and bring to the boil. Turn down the heat, half-cover the pan and simmer gently for at least 2 hours, topping up with more stock as necessary, until the meat is very tender and the sauce thick and reduced. Season to taste with salt and pepper and remove the bay leaves before serving.

30
PREP

140
COOK

4
SERVES

rich

1 **hare**, skinned and jointed

3 tablespoons **olive oil**

50 g (2 oz) **butter**

1 **onion**, finely diced

1 **carrot**, finely diced

1 **celery stick**, finely diced

2 **garlic cloves**, chopped

75 g (3 oz) **unsmoked pancetta**, diced

2 tablespoons **plain flour**

300 ml (½ pint) dry **red wine**

about 600 ml (1 pint) **chicken stock** (see page 19)

1 teaspoon chopped **rosemary**

1 tablespoon chopped **sage**

2 **bay leaves**

salt and **pepper**

500 g (1 lb) **rabbit**, jointed

2 tablespoons **olive oil**

1 **onion**, chopped

1 **celery stick**, chopped

1 **carrot**, diced

125 g (4 oz) **pancetta** or **bacon**, diced

2 **garlic cloves**, crushed

1 tablespoon **plain flour**

1 tablespoon **tomato purée**

150 ml (¼ pint) **red wine**

150 ml (¼ pint) **chicken stock** (see page 19)

400 g (13 oz) can **chopped tomatoes**

1 tablespoon chopped **parsley**

½ teaspoon dried **oregano**

pinch of **nutmeg**

salt and **pepper**

50 g (2 oz) **Parmesan cheese**, freshly grated, to serve

20
PREP

90
COOK

4
SERVES

rich

Rabbit and red wine sauce

Rabbit is quite easy to find in the super-market or your local butcher these days. If you can't get hold of any, or don't like it, you can use skinless chicken instead. Serve with tagliatelle or pappardelle.

1 Cut all the meat off the rabbit bones and chop fairly finely. Heat the oil in a pan and fry the onion, celery, carrot and pancetta or bacon for 6–7 minutes.

2 Add the meat, garlic, flour and tomato purée. Gently fry for 15 minutes, then add the wine. Bring to the boil, then reduce the heat and simmer for a few minutes, then add the stock, tomatoes, herbs and nutmeg. Simmer gently for 1 hour or until the meat is tender and the mixture fairly thick. Season to taste with salt and pepper and serve with grated Parmesan.

Rich rabbit sauce

10
PREP

130
COOK

4
SERVES

hearty

You can replace the rabbit with four chicken joints if you prefer. The long cooking time helps the meat to tenderize beautifully and soak up all the flavours of the sauce. Serve with conchiglie.

1 Heat the oil in a large saucepan, add the onion, carrot and celery and fry for about 2–3 minutes until softened. Add the rabbit or chicken and fry for 2–3 minutes until browned all over, then add the spice and flour and stir to combine.

2 Add the orange rind, rosemary sprig and marjoram, then gradually stir in the wine and stock. Bring the mixture to the boil, then cover, reduce the heat and simmer for about 2 hours until the rabbit or chicken is tender. Carefully remove all the bones, returning any rabbit flesh to the pan. Add the crème fraîche and stir to combine.

1 teaspoon **olive oil**

1 **onion**, chopped

1 **carrot**, finely chopped

1 **celery stick**, diced

1 **rabbit**, jointed, or 4 chicken joints

1 teaspoon **five spice powder**

1 tablespoon **plain flour**

pared **rind of 1 orange**

1 sprig of **rosemary**

1 teaspoon chopped **marjoram**

300 ml (½ pint) **red wine**

300 ml (½ pint) **beef stock** (see page 20)

4 tablespoons reduced-fat **crème fraîche**

pepper

25 g (1 oz) **butter**

1 **onion**, finely chopped

2 **garlic cloves**, crushed

250 g (8 oz) **mushrooms**, sliced

500 g (1 lb) lean minced **beef**

600 ml (1 pint) **beef stock** (see page 20)

2 tablespoons **tomato purée**

300 ml (½ pint) **soured cream**

salt and **pepper**

2 tablespoons chopped **parsley**, to garnish

10

PREP

20

COOK

4

SERVES

meaty

Stroganoff sauce

This recipe is all about the meat, so choose the best possible quality and ask your butcher to mince it for you. Serve with penne pasta, as it's a chunky sauce.

1 Melt the butter in a large saucepan, add the onion and garlic and fry for about 5 minutes until softened. Add the mushrooms and cook for another minute.

2 Crumble over the meat and cook, stirring frequently, until it is no longer pink. Add the stock and tomato purée, mixing well. Bring to the boil, reduce the heat and simmer for 10 minutes.

3 Stir the soured cream into the meat sauce and season with salt and pepper to taste. Serve garnished with parsley.

Ham and mushroom sauce

Ham and mushrooms make a really great combination, and the addition of double cream and cheese results in a really creamy flavour. Gnocchi would be the ideal accompaniment, as its light, floury texture would work perfectly with the sauce.

1 Melt the butter in a large saucepan. Add the mushrooms and ham and fry for about 5 minutes until softened.

2 Mix together the cream and cheese and stir into the mushroom and ham mixture along with the parsley and olives. Stir gently over a low heat until slightly thickened, then season to taste with salt and pepper. Serve with grated Parmesan.

10
PREP

8
COOK

4
SERVES

easy

25 g (1 oz) **butter**

125 g (4 oz) **mushrooms**, sliced

175 g (6 oz) cooked **ham**, cut into matchstick strips

150 ml (¼ pint) **double cream**

175 g (6 oz) **Cheddar cheese**, freshly grated

1 tablespoon finely chopped **parsley**

handful of pitted **black olives**

salt and **pepper**

2 tablespoons freshly grated **Parmesan cheese**, to serve

40 g (1½ oz) **butter**

1 tablespoon **olive oil**

3 **garlic cloves**, finely chopped

175 g (6 oz) cooked **ham**, finely diced

400 g (13 oz) can **chopped tomatoes**

salt and **pepper**

TO SERVE:

2 tablespoons chopped **basil**

100 g (4 oz) **pecorino cheese** or **Parmesan cheese**, freshly grated

10

PREP

20

COOK

4

SERVES

easy

Ham, tomato and cheese sauce

This quick and easy sauce is perfect for speedy midweek meals. Try serving with macaroni. If you combine the sauce and pasta in an ovenproof dish and then sprinkle over the cheese, you can pop it under a hot grill for a couple of minutes to melt the cheese.

1 Heat the butter and oil in a saucepan over a medium heat. Add the garlic and ham and fry gently for 4–5 minutes.

2 Add the tomatoes and bring the mixture to the boil, then reduce the heat and simmer for about 10–15 minutes, or until it is well blended, stirring frequently. Season to taste with salt and pepper.

3 Mix the basil with the cheese and sprinkle over the sauce.

Red sauce with peas

Another easy sauce that just needs to simmer slowly. The bacon will add a gorgeous smoked flavour, and the peas will liven up the sauce with their vibrant colour.

1 Melt the butter in a saucepan and cook the bacon over a medium heat. Before it becomes crisp, add the peas and leave to flavour for 2 minutes.

2 Add the tomatoes to the pan, pour in the stock and cook over a low heat for 30 minutes, stirring from time to time to prevent the sauce from sticking to the pan. Season to taste with salt and pepper.

10
PREP

35
COOK

4
SERVES

gutsy

50 g (2 oz) **butter**

125 g (4 oz) **smoked bacon**, rind removed and diced

125 g (4 oz) frozen **peas**

500 g (1 lb) **plum tomatoes**, skinned (see page 16) and roughly chopped

250 ml (8 fl oz) **vegetable stock** (see page 21)

salt and **pepper**

vegetarian

2 tablespoons **olive oil**

1 **onion**, finely chopped

2 **garlic cloves**, chopped

2 x 400 g (13 oz) cans **chopped tomatoes**

250 ml (8 fl oz) **red wine**

50–125 g (2–4 oz) pitted **Kalamata olives**, roughly chopped

salt and **pepper**

Parmesan cheese shavings, to serve (optional)

15

PREP

35

COOK

4

SERVES

rustic

Black olive and tomato sauce

Kalamata olives are large black olives that are grown around Kalamata in Greece. They have a meaty texture and a delicious, strong flavour that is essential for this sauce.

1 Heat 1 tablespoon of the olive oil in a large, heavy-based saucepan, add the onion, cover and cook gently for 10 minutes, stirring from time to time. Stir in the garlic and cook for 1–2 minutes longer.

2 Add the tomatoes and wine to the pan. Bring to the boil, reduce the heat and leave to simmer, uncovered, stirring from time to time, for 20 minutes or until thick.

3 Liquidize the sauce in a food processor or blender or use a stick blender and return it to the saucepan. Stir in the olives, season with salt and pepper and reheat. Serve with Parmesan shavings, if using.

Olive and sun-dried tomato sauce

These sun-dried tomatoes are stored in oil so they don't need rehydrating before use. The flavour is concentrated so you don't need a large amount to make a big difference to the finished sauce.

10
PREP

10
COOK

4
SERVES

quick

1 Cook the peas in lightly salted boiling water for 5 minutes.

2 Heat the oil in a large, nonstick frying pan. Add the garlic, shallots, green pepper and peas and fry for about 5 minutes until the onions are light brown and the peppers are cooked.

3 Add the mint, basil, tomatoes, olives and capers. Season to taste with salt and pepper. Heat through and stir in the crème fraîche.

125 g (4 oz) **peas**

1 tablespoon **olive oil**

2 **garlic cloves**, crushed

4 **shallots**, finely chopped

1 **green pepper**, cored, deseeded and diced

15 g (½ oz) **mint**, chopped

25 g (1 oz) **basil leaves**, chopped

125 g (4 oz) **sun-dried tomatoes** in oil, drained and sliced

50 g (2 oz) pitted **black olives**

1 tablespoon **capers**, chopped

150 ml (¼ pint) reduced-fat **crème fraîche**

salt and **pepper**

3 tablespoons chopped **mint**

½ tablespoon chopped **flat leaf parsley**

½ **garlic clove**, chopped

½ tablespoon freshly grated **Parmesan cheese**

½ tablespoon **double cream**

½ teaspoon **balsamic vinegar**

1–2 tablespoons extra virgin **olive oil**

salt and **pepper**

5

PREP

0

COOK

4

SERVES

herby

Mint pesto

This variation of the classic pesto sauce has a wonderfully summery, fresh flavour because of the mint and parsley. The cream and balsamic vinegar add contrasting hits of sweet and sour, which make this a perfectly balanced combination.

1 Place all of the ingredients in a food processor or blender and blend until fairly smooth. Season to taste with salt and pepper.

Pesto sauce with green olives

Walnuts are used instead of the traditional pine nuts in this no-cook pasta sauce that would work well on hot pasta or as a salad accompaniment. It also makes a lovely dip, served with crudités or warm bread.

1 Put the garlic, walnuts and olives in a food processor and process until finely chopped. Add the basil leaves and olive oil and blend until smooth.

2 Scrape the sauce into a bowl, stir in the lemon juice and pecorino or Parmesan, and season to taste with salt and pepper. Serve with basil leaves and extra cheese, if liked.

7

PREP

0

COOK

4

SERVES

nutty

1 small **garlic clove**

25 g (1 oz) shelled **walnuts**

100 g (3½ oz) pitted **green olives**

1 large bunch of **basil**, leaves stripped, plus extra for serving

3–4 tablespoons extra virgin **olive oil**

1 tablespoon **lemon juice**

50 g (2 oz) **pecorino cheese** or **Parmesan cheese**, freshly grated, plus extra for serving (optional)

salt and **pepper**

400 g (13 oz) can **chickpeas**, drained and rinsed

6 tablespoons **olive oil**

1 small **onion**, finely chopped

1 **celery stick**, diced

2 **garlic cloves**, finely chopped

1½ x 400 g (13 oz) cans **chopped tomatoes**

2 tablespoons chopped **flat leaf parsley**

1 teaspoon finely chopped **rosemary**

salt and **pepper**

4 tablespoons freshly grated **Parmesan cheese**, to serve

20
PREP

25
COOK

4
SERVES

hearty

Chickpea and tomato sauce

Chickpeas produce a hearty, textured sauce and this recipe will delight hummus fans, as they are the dip's main ingredient. Leaving some whole gives a chunky finish.

1 Purée half the chickpeas in a blender, adding a little water if necessary.

2 Heat the oil and gently fry the onion and celery until just soft. Add the garlic and fry until just beginning to colour.

3 Add the tomatoes, parsley and rosemary, bring to the boil, then reduce the heat and simmer for 10–15 minutes until thickened. Stir in the puréed and whole chickpeas and simmer for another 5 minutes. Season to taste with salt and pepper and serve with grated Parmesan.

Tomato and egg sauce

This tomato sauce is a great staple and you might like to make extra and keep it in the freezer to use later. The eggs and cheese help thicken the sauce and add a creamy texture.

8

PREP

12

COOK

4

SERVES

thick

2 **eggs**

25 g (1 oz) **Parmesan cheese**, freshly grated

4 tablespoons **mascarpone cheese** or **single cream**

salt and **pepper**

basil leaves, to garnish

TOMATO SAUCE:

425 g (14 oz) jar **passata** (sieved tomatoes)

1 **garlic clove**, crushed

2 tablespoons **olive oil**

½ teaspoon **caster sugar**

1 **bay leaf**

1 tablespoon chopped **basil**

1 Place all the tomato sauce ingredients in a saucepan and bring to the boil. Cover, reduce the heat and simmer for 10 minutes. Taste and adjust the seasoning, if necessary, then discard the bay leaf and keep the sauce warm.

2 Beat together the eggs, Parmesan and mascarpone or cream until evenly combined. Season with salt and pepper.

3 Remove the tomato sauce from the heat and whisk in the egg mixture. Garnish with basil leaves.

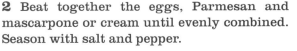

2 tablespoons **olive oil**

1 **garlic clove**, chopped

2 **shallots**, chopped

125 g (4 oz) shelled **peas**

125 g (4 oz) shelled young **broad beans**, skinned

125 g (4 oz) **asparagus**, trimmed and cut into 5 cm (2 inch) lengths

125 g (4 oz) **spinach**, washed and chopped

150 ml (¼ pint) **whipping cream**

salt and **pepper**

handful of **mint leaves**, chopped, to garnish

75 g (3 oz) **Parmesan cheese**, grated, to serve

15
PREP

8
COOK

4
SERVES

fresh

Salsa primavera verde

This recipe uses small, young broad beans. If only the large, mature broad beans are available, shell, skin and cook them first. Toss the sauce with green and white tagliatelle to complete the colour scheme.

1 Heat the oil in a saucepan and sauté the garlic and shallots for 3 minutes. Add the peas, broad beans, asparagus and spinach to the shallot mixture. Stir well and cook for 2 minutes.

2 Stir the cream into the vegetables and mix well. Bring to the boil, then reduce the heat and simmer for 3 minutes. Season to taste with salt and pepper. Garnish with mint and serve with grated Parmesan.

Fresh tomato and soya bolognese

A fresh tomato sauce is an ideal base for soya mince or pieces, as well as cooked soya beans or pieces of fried firm tofu. Gently simmer together and serve with egg pasta.

1 Heat the oil in a large saucepan, add the onion and cook for about 4–5 minutes until softened and golden-brown. Add the garlic and cook for 1–2 minutes, but do not allow the garlic to burn.

2 Add the red wine to the pan, then add the tomatoes, tomato purée, soy sauce, the whole carrot, bay leaf and thyme and bring slowly to the boil. Stir well, then reduce the heat and leave to simmer for 25 minutes.

3 Add the soya mince to the tomato sauce with the torn basil leaves and simmer gently for 5–10 minutes. Remove the whole carrot and thyme stalks and season to taste with salt and pepper. Garnish with basil and serve with Parmesan shavings.

30
PREP

45
COOK

4
SERVES

gutsy

2 tablespoons **olive oil**

1 **onion**, finely chopped

1 **garlic clove**

150 ml (¼ pint) **red wine**

1 kg (2 lb) ripe **tomatoes**, skinned (see page 16) and chopped or 2 x 400 g (13 oz) cans **chopped tomatoes**

1 tablespoon **tomato purée**

1 tablespoon **soy sauce**

1 **carrot**

1 **bay leaf**

2 sprigs of **thyme**

500 g (1 lb) **dried soya mince** or **dried soya pieces**, prepared according to packet instructions

2 tablespoons torn **basil leaves**

salt and **pepper**

basil leaves, to garnish

Parmesan cheese shavings, to serve

1 tablespoon **vegetable oil**

1 **onion**, chopped

1 **garlic clove**, crushed

150 g (5 oz) **dried soya mince**, prepared according to packet instructions

125 g (4 oz) **mushrooms**, sliced

1 **carrot**, sliced

1 kg (2 lb) ripe **tomatoes**, skinned (see page 16) and chopped, or 2 x 400 g (13 oz) cans **chopped tomatoes**

150 ml (¼ pint) **vegetable stock** (see page 21)

2 tablespoons **tomato purée**

1 teaspoon **dried oregano**

1 teaspoon **dried basil**

1 teaspoon **yeast extract**

pepper

freshly grated **Parmesan cheese**, to serve

15

PREP

30

COOK

4

SERVES

hearty

Tomato and mushroom soya bolognese

Vegetarians need not miss out on the joys of spaghetti Bolognese with this hearty recipe. The herbs add extra flavour and the mushrooms add some bulk to this delicious, rich wintry dish.

1 Heat the oil in a large saucepan, add the onion and garlic and cook, stirring, for 2–3 minutes until softened.

2 Add the remaining ingredients, stir well and bring to the boil, then reduce the heat and simmer for 20–25 minutes. Season to taste with salt and pepper, then serve with grated Parmesan.

Lentil and tomato sauce

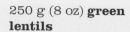

10

PREP

60

COOK

4

SERVES

rustic

Keep checking the lentils as they cook, because the cooking time will vary according to their age and condition of storage. For a particularly sumptuous version of this dish, use puy lentils, the caviar of lentils!

250 g (8 oz) **green lentils**

1 tablespoon **olive oil**

1 **onion**, chopped

2 **garlic cloves**, crushed

400 g (13 oz) can **plum tomatoes**

2 tablespoons **tomato purée**

600 ml (1 pint) **vegetable stock** (see page 21)

salt and **pepper**

1 tablespoon chopped **basil**, to garnish

1 Bring a large saucepan of water to the boil. Add the lentils and boil rapidly for 10 minutes. Drain them and set aside.

2 Meanwhile, heat the oil in a large frying pan. Add the onion and garlic and fry, stirring constantly, for 3–5 minutes until softened but not coloured.

3 Add the lentils. Stir-fry for 1 minute, then stir in the tomatoes with the can juices, the tomato purée and stock. Bring to the boil, then reduce the heat and simmer, uncovered, for 45 minutes until reduced by half, stirring occasionally to break up the tomatoes. Season to taste with salt and pepper and garnish with basil.

1 tablespoon **olive oil**

1 **onion**, chopped

250 g (8 oz) **carrots**, diced

1 **leek**, sliced

2 **celery sticks**, sliced

400 g (13 oz) can **plum tomatoes**, drained and roughly chopped

1 tablespoon **tomato purée**

1 teaspoon **cayenne pepper**

125 g (4 oz) **mushrooms**, sliced

salt and **pepper**

basil leaves, to garnish

PREP **15**

COOK **15**

SERVES **4**

feast

Vegetable bolognese

This sauce is packed full of tasty vegetables. Blitz the sauce briefly in a food processor to make a smoother consistency, if preferred.

1 Heat the oil in a large saucepan and fry the onion and carrots for 3–5 minutes.

2 Add the remaining ingredients, bring to the boil, then reduce the heat and simmer for 10 minutes. Season to taste with salt and pepper, then garnish with basil.

Buttery tomato sauce

10
PREP

25
COOK

4
SERVES

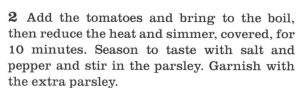

simple

This is a very easy sauce to make. Unsalted butter is used as this allows you to season the sauce to your liking at the end. Plum tomatoes have a really intense flavour so don't substitute them for a different variety in this particular recipe.

1 Melt the butter in a large frying pan and add the onion, garlic and salt and pepper. Cook over a low heat for 10 minutes until the onion rings are translucent but not browned.

2 Add the tomatoes and bring to the boil, then reduce the heat and simmer, covered, for 10 minutes. Season to taste with salt and pepper and stir in the parsley. Garnish with the extra parsley.

125 g (4 oz) **unsalted butter**

1 **onion**, sliced into rings

2 **garlic cloves**, crushed

1 kg (2 lb) ripe **plum tomatoes**, skinned (see page 16), deseeded and chopped

2 tablespoons chopped **parsley**, plus extra to garnish

salt and **pepper**

1 large **onion**, chopped

1 **garlic clove**, crushed

500 g (1 lb) **courgettes**, sliced

1 large **aubergine**, diced

1 **green pepper**, cored, deseeded and diced

500 g (1 lb) **tomatoes**, skinned (see page 16) and chopped

1 tablespoon chopped **oregano** or **basil**

salt and **pepper**

1 tablespoon chopped **parsley**, to garnish

20

PREP

35

COOK

4

SERVES

hearty

Ratatouille sauce

This sauce could be used as an alternative sauce in vegetarian lasagne. Otherwise, serve with a ridged pasta, such as penne.

1 Put all the ingredients into a large saucepan. Add enough water to cover the vegetables, bring to the boil, then reduce the heat and simmer, stirring occasionally, for 30 minutes until the vegetables are tender and the juices have thickened slightly.

2 Season to taste with salt and pepper, then garnish with parsley.

Vegetable ragoût sauce

10
PREP

25
COOK

Red pesto gets its colour from sun-dried tomatoes. It's quite easy to make your own, or you can use a bought jar. Pesto can start to dry out once it's opened; add a trickle of olive oil if this happens.

4
SERVES

1 Heat the oil in a saucepan, add the garlic and onion and fry for about 3–5 minutes, until softened. Add the carrot and celery and fry for 5 minutes more. Stir in the red pepper, salt and pepper. Fry for a further 10 minutes, adding a little water if necessary.

2 Add the tomatoes and pesto to the red pepper mixture. Cook for 5 minutes, taste and add more salt and pepper if required. Garnish with parsley.

rich

1 tablespoon **olive oil**

2 **garlic cloves**, crushed

1 **onion**, chopped

1 **carrot**, finely chopped

1 **celery stick**, chopped

1 **red pepper**, cored, deseeded and chopped

4 ripe **plum tomatoes**, chopped

3 tablespoons **red pesto**

salt and **pepper**

2 tablespoons chopped **parsley**, to garnish

1 tablespoon **olive oil**

1 **onion**, finely chopped

2 **garlic cloves**, crushed

1 tablespoon **Madras curry powder**

2 tablespoons **tomato purée**

400 g (13 oz) can **chopped tomatoes**

2 teaspoons **garam masala**

2 tablespoons chopped fresh **coriander leaves**, plus some whole leaves, to garnish

10

PREP

15

COOK

4

SERVES

spicy

Curried tomato sauce

This unusual recipe combines elements of Indian cuisine, with the addition of curry powder, garam masala and coriander. Garam masala is a blend of different spices, and it varies from region to region in India.

1 Heat the oil in a frying pan, add the onion and garlic and fry for 3–5 minutes, until the onion has softened.

2 Stir in the curry powder, tomato purée and the chopped tomatoes. Bring to the boil, then reduce the heat and simmer, uncovered, for 5–10 minutes.

3 Sprinkle in the garam masala, followed by the chopped coriander, and stir well. Garnish with whole coriander leaves.

Creamy walnut sauce

15

PREP

5

COOK

4–6

SERVES

nutty

300 ml (½ pint) **milk**

2 slices of **wholemeal bread**, crusts removed

300 g (10 oz) **walnut pieces**

1 **garlic clove**, crushed

50 g (2 oz) **Parmesan cheese**, freshly grated, plus extra to serve

100 ml (3½ fl oz) **olive oil**

150 ml (¼ pint) **double cream**

salt and **pepper**

For an even richer sauce, why not add 125 g (4 oz) pitted black oven-dried olives to the ingredients in the food processor?

1 Pour the milk into a shallow dish, add the bread slices and leave to soak until all of the milk has been absorbed.

2 Meanwhile, spread out the walnuts on a baking sheet and roast in a preheated oven, 190°C (375°F), Gas Mark 5, for 5 minutes. Set aside to cool.

3 Put the bread, walnuts, garlic, Parmesan and olive oil into a food processor and blend until smooth. Season to taste with salt and pepper, then stir in the double cream. Serve with the extra grated Parmesan.

1 tablespoon **olive oil**

50 ml (2 fl oz) **double cream**

25 g (1 oz) **Cheddar cheese**, grated

25 g (1 oz) **walnuts**, finely chopped

25 g (1 oz) fresh **coriander**, finely chopped, plus extra sprigs to garnish

salt and **pepper**

5

PREP

0

COOK

4

SERVES

nutty

Coriander and walnut sauce

This sauce can be made in advance and stored in the refrigerator in a covered container for one or two days.

1 Place the olive oil and cream in a bowl. Add the cheese, walnuts and chopped coriander.

2 Mix the ingredients together thoroughly, then season to taste with salt and pepper. Garnish with sprigs of coriander.

Garlic, roasted pepper and walnut sauce

Roasting the peppers first intensifies the flavour. To remove the blackened skins, place the peppers in a freezer bag for a couple of minutes to sweat. Then run them under a cold tap and the skins should rub off easily.

15

PREP

30

COOK

4

SERVES

rustic

2 teaspoons **olive oil**

4 **red peppers**, cored, deseeded and sliced

3–4 large **garlic cloves**, thinly sliced

60 g (2½ oz) **walnuts**, chopped

25 g (1 oz) **Parmesan cheese**, shaved

salt and **pepper**

1 Brush ½ teaspoon of the olive oil over the peppers. Put the peppers on a baking sheet and roast them in a preheated oven, 230°C (450°F), Gas Mark 8, for 20–25 minutes until they are soft and just beginning to blacken.

2 Reserve 4 slices of the pepper to use as a garnish and cut the remaining peppers into large dice.

3 Heat the remaining olive oil in a large frying pan and fry the sliced garlic without letting it brown. Add the diced red pepper and stir in the walnuts. Season to taste with salt and pepper. Garnish with the reserved pepper slices and serve with Parmesan shavings

50 g (2 oz) **butter**

1 tablespoon **olive oil**

1 **onion**, very finely chopped

250 g (8 oz) **radicchio**, finely shredded, few small inner leaves reserved for garnish

150 ml (¼ pint) **double cream**

50 g (2 oz) **Parmesan cheese**, freshly grated

salt and **pepper**

10

PREP

15

COOK

4

SERVES

fresh

Radicchio and cream sauce

This sauce is best served fresh. Radicchio has a slightly bitter taste that will be well complemented by the cream and cheese in this recipe. It is very popular in Italian cuisine, where it is eaten in salads, or grilled.

1 Melt the butter with the oil in a large, heavy-based saucepan. Add the onion and cook gently for about 10 minutes, stirring frequently, until softened.

2 Add the shredded radicchio and cook, stirring, over a moderate heat, until it wilts and begins to turn brown. Stir in the cream and heat it through. Season to taste with salt and pepper. Garnish with the curly radicchio leaves and serve with grated Parmesan.

Roasted pepper, coriander and chilli pesto

20 PREP

The chilli adds a lively kick to this unusual pesto sauce. If you like a real punch use a bird's eye chilli. Otherwise, choose a larger red or green chilli. The seeds carry the most heat so, again, if you like it hot, you can keep some of these in the sauce.

50 COOK

1 Roast the peppers in a preheated oven, 220°C (425°F), Gas Mark 7, until the skins blacken on all sides. Remove from the oven, remove the skins and seeds, then chop the flesh into 1 cm (½ inch) dice.

2 Put the coriander and chillies in a blender or food processor with the garlic, pine nuts, lime rind and salt. Purée until smooth, gradually adding the olive oil. Transfer to a bowl and mix with the roasted peppers and Parmesan cheese.

4 SERVES

hot

3 mixed **red and yellow peppers**

50 g (2 oz) trimmed fresh **coriander** leaves and stems, roughly chopped

1 **chilli**, deseeded and roughly chopped

2 **garlic cloves**, crushed

2 tablespoons **pine nuts**

finely grated **rind of 1 lime**

1 teaspoon **salt**

8 tablespoons **olive oil**

50 g (2 oz) **Parmesan cheese**, freshly grated

3 large **red peppers**, cored, deseeded and roughly chopped

1 **yellow pepper** or **orange pepper**, cored, deseeded and roughly chopped

1 **red onion**, chopped

2 **garlic cloves**, sliced

3 **tomatoes**, skinned (see page 16) and quartered

4 large sprigs of **oregano**, roughly chopped

5 tablespoons **olive oil**

5 tablespoons **white wine** or **water**

salt and **pepper**

15

PREP

50

COOK

4

SERVES

sweet

Roasted pepper sauce

Unlike most sauces, this one's baked in the oven until it's sweet and caramelized before it's lightly blended to a fine consistency. It's delicious served as it is with spaghetti or linguini, or with some chopped mozzarella stirred in just before serving.

1 Put the peppers, onion, garlic, tomatoes and oregano into a large roasting tin. Drizzle with 3 tablespoons of the olive oil and a little salt and pepper and toss the ingredients together well. Roast in a preheated oven, 220°C (425°F), Gas Mark 7, for 50 minutes until the vegetables are thoroughly browned around the edges. Turn the ingredients once or twice during roasting.

2 Tip the mixture into a food processor or a blender. Stir the white wine or water into the roasting tin to scrape up the pan juices and add to the pepper mixture. Blend very lightly so the vegetables become chopped and pulpy.

3 Return the sauce to the roasting tin with the remaining oil and reheat for 2 minutes. Check the seasoning and serve hot.

Sweet spicy aubergine sauce

Aubergines contain a lot of moisture. To draw this out, cut them into large slices, lay them flat in a colander and sprinkle with salt. Leave for about 30 minutes, then pat dry and chop them into cubes.

1 Heat the oil in a large saucepan. Add the sesame or poppy seeds with the onion. Fry for 2 minutes, then add the red pepper, aubergines and chilli and fry for 5 minutes, stirring constantly.

2 Stir in the tomato purée, measured water and vinegar. Bring to the boil, then reduce the heat and simmer the sauce for about 10 minutes. Season to taste with salt and pepper, then stir in the coriander.

15 PREP

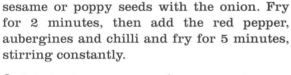

20 COOK

4 SERVES

spicy

1½ tablespoons **olive oil**

1 teaspoon **sesame seeds** or **poppy seeds**

1 **onion**, finely chopped

1 **red pepper**, cored, deseeded and chopped

250 g (8 oz) **aubergines**, chopped

½ **red chilli**, deseeded and chopped

2 tablespoons **tomato purée**

50 ml (2 fl oz) **water**

1 tablespoon **cider vinegar**

2 tablespoons chopped fresh **coriander**

salt and **pepper**

250 g (8 oz) **cherry tomatoes**, halved

sea salt

2 teaspoons **pesto**

4 tablespoons **olive oil**

2 **spring onions**, finely sliced

1 **chilli**, deseeded and finely chopped

2 **garlic cloves**

1 tablespoon **raspberry vinegar**

1 tablespoon **orange juice**

2 tablespoons toasted **hazelnuts**, chopped

2 tablespoons chopped **basil**, plus extra, shredded, to garnish

salt

125 g (4 oz) **Parmesan cheese**, freshly grated, to serve

10

PREP

15

COOK

4

SERVES

subtle

Chilli and roast cherry tomato sauce

If you can't find raspberry vinegar you could use white wine or cider vinegar in this recipe. The raspberry flavour and orange juice give the sauce a subtle, fruity flavour.

1 Arrange the tomatoes on a baking sheet. Sprinkle with a little sea salt, top with the pesto and drizzle with 1 tablespoon of the oil, then toss carefully, making sure you coat the tomatoes well. Cook in a preheated oven, 200°C (400°F), Gas Mark 6, for 15 minutes.

2 Meanwhile, heat the remaining oil in a small saucepan. Add the spring onions, chilli and garlic and fry for 1 minute, stirring continuously. Remove from the heat and add the vinegar, orange juice, nuts and basil. Stir well and season to taste with salt.

3 Carefully stir the tomatoes into the onion mixture, then garnish with shredded basil and serve with grated Parmesan.

Fresh tomato and basil sauce

This is a classic Italian combination that is found in many pasta and pizza recipes. It's a simple partnership of two wonderfully fresh, flavoursome ingredients, and it works well with any pasta.

1 Place all the ingredients in a saucepan and bring to the boil. Reduce the heat, cover and simmer gently for 30 minutes.

2 Remove the lid and simmer for a further 20 minutes until the sauce is thick. Season with salt and pepper to taste.

10
PREP

50
COOK

4
SERVES

classic

1 kg (2 lb) ripe **tomatoes**, skinned (see page 16) and roughly chopped

2 tablespoons **olive oil**

2 **garlic cloves**, chopped

2 tablespoons chopped **basil**

1 teaspoon grated **lemon rind**

pinch of **caster sugar**

salt and **pepper**

3 tablespoons **olive oil**

2 **garlic cloves**, crushed

2 **red chillies**, deseeded and chopped

4 tablespoons **balsamic vinegar**

2 tablespoons **orange juice**

3 tablespoons **red pesto**

1 bunch of **spring onions**, shredded

25 g (1 oz) toasted **hazelnuts**, chopped

salt

2 tablespoons chopped **mixed herbs**, to garnish

10

PREP

4

COOK

4

SERVES

nutty

Chilli balsamic sauce

This recipe uses quite a large quantity of balsamic vinegar so choose a good quality bottle. The hazelnuts will add a nutty, smoky flavour and a nice rough texture. Overall, a delicious yet unusual combination.

1 Heat the oil in a saucepan. Add the garlic and chillies and fry for 2 minutes.

2 Reduce the heat, stir in the remaining ingredients and heat through. Garnish with mixed herbs.

Guacamole sauce

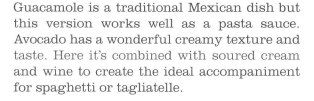

Guacamole is a traditional Mexican dish but this version works well as a pasta sauce. Avocado has a wonderful creamy texture and taste. Here it's combined with soured cream and wine to create the ideal accompaniment for spaghetti or tagliatelle.

1 Heat the oil in a heavy-based saucepan. Add the onion, celery and diced pepper and cook gently, stirring frequently, for about 10 minutes until softened. Add the oregano or marjoram, chilli powder and garlic and stir over a gentle heat for 1–2 minutes until the ingredients are mixed.

2 Add the tomatoes and wine and stir. Bring to the boil, then cover, reduce the heat and simmer for 15 minutes, stirring occasionally. Season to taste with salt and pepper.

3 Meanwhile, halve, pit and then peel the avocado. Dice the flesh and sprinkle it with the lemon juice to prevent discoloration.

4 Remove the sauce from the heat and stir in the avocado and half the soured cream or yogurt. Taste and adjust the seasoning if necessary. Garnish with marjoram and serve with the remaining soured cream or yogurt spooned on top.

20

PREP

30

COOK

4

SERVES

gutsy

3 tablespoons **olive oil**

1 small **onion**, finely chopped

2 **celery sticks**, finely chopped

1 **red pepper** or **green pepper**, cored, deseeded and finely diced

2 teaspoons chopped **oregano** or **marjoram**

½–1 teaspoon **chilli powder**, according to taste

1–2 **garlic cloves**, crushed

500 g (1 lb) ripe **tomatoes**, skinned (see page 16), deseeded and chopped, or 400 g (13 oz) can **chopped tomatoes**

150 ml (¼ pint) dry **white wine**

1 large ripe **avocado**

2 tablespoons **lemon juice**

150 ml (¼ pint) **soured cream** or Greek yogurt

salt and **pepper**

sprigs of **marjoram**, to garnish

vegetarian **125**

1 ripe **avocado**, halved and pitted

4 tablespoons **lemon juice**

1 **garlic clove**, crushed

1 teaspoon **caster sugar**

150 ml (¼ pint) **single cream**

salt and **pepper**

TO GARNISH:

4 **spring onions**, chopped

2 tablespoons chopped **parsley**

15

PREP

0

COOK

6–8

SERVES

simple

Avocado and cream sauce

This simple, no-cook sauce would be perfect for a quick lunch or as a pasta salad side dish. Conchiglie or fusilli would be good choices for the pasta, as they will hold the creamy sauce. Remember to mix the pasta and sauce well before serving.

1 Scoop the avocado flesh out of the skin and place in a blender or food processor with the lemon juice, garlic, sugar and cream. Purée until smooth. Season the sauce to taste with salt and pepper.

2 Garnish with spring onions and parsley and serve lightly chilled.

Rocket, garlic and chilli sauce

With just a few ingredients, this sauce depends on the vibrant colour and distinctive flavour of the rocket for its success. It has a light, fresh taste and would work well as a healthy lunch dish, if served with whole-wheat fusilli.

1 Heat the oil and gently fry the garlic and chilli flakes until the garlic begins to colour.

2 Add the rocket and stir until just wilted. Season to taste with salt and pepper, then serve with grated Parmesan.

10

PREP

5

COOK

4

SERVES

easy

8 tablespoons **olive oil**

3 **garlic cloves**, finely chopped

½ teaspoon **dried chilli flakes**

100 g (4 oz) **rocket**, roughly chopped

salt and **pepper**

50 g (2 oz) **Parmesan cheese**, freshly grated, to serve

1 teaspoon **sunflower oil**

1 small **onion**, finely chopped

125 g (4 oz) **mushrooms**, sliced

400 g (13 oz) can **plum tomatoes**

1 tablespoon chopped **basil** (optional)

salt and **pepper**

5

PREP

25

COOK

2

SERVES

simple

Tomato and mushroom sauce

This simple dish is ideal for children, who will enjoy it even more if it is made with little pasta shapes. Blitz the sauce in the food processor briefly for fussy eaters!

1 Heat the oil in a saucepan, add the onion and mushrooms and sauté for 5 minutes.

2 Stir in the tomatoes, bring to the boil, then reduce the heat and simmer, uncovered, for 15 minutes to reduce the sauce. Add the basil, if using, and simmer for a further 5 minutes. Season to taste with salt and pepper.

Broad beans and greens sauce

This is a real summer dish, using delicious seasonal broad beans and greens. It packs a bit of a healthy punch too and can be served hot or cold. Penne or rigatoni would be good choices for this sauce.

15
PREP

20
COOK

4
SERVES

fresh

1 Plunge the broad beans into boiling water for about 2 minutes. Drain them under cold running water, then slip off the outer skins if they are tough.

2 Heat the oil in a large saucepan and gently fry the onion until just soft. Add the garlic, sage and chilli flakes.

3 Add the greens and toss the leaves until they are coated with oil. Cover and cook over a medium heat for 7–10 minutes, until the greens are just tender, adding a little water if the mixture gets too dry. Stir in the beans and season to taste. Stir in the Parmesan cheese.

250 g (8 oz) shelled young **broad beans**

6 tablespoons **olive oil**

1 **red onion**, finely chopped

3 **garlic cloves**, finely chopped

3 **sage leaves**, finely chopped

½ teaspoon **dried chilli flakes**

750 g (1½ lb) **spring greens**, **kale** or **Swiss chard**, tough stalks removed and finely sliced

salt and **pepper**

4 tablespoons freshly grated **Parmesan cheese**

500 g (1 lb) **courgettes**, cut into matchstick strips

5 tablespoons **olive oil**

2 **onions**, very thinly sliced

1 **garlic clove**, finely chopped

1 tablespoon finely chopped **flat leaf parsley**

2 tablespoons finely chopped **rosemary**

50 g (2 oz) **Parmesan cheese**, freshly grated

salt and **pepper**

75
PREP

10
COOK

4–6
SERVES

herby

Courgette sauce with rosemary

Garlic and courgette are a great combination as they complement each other very well. Sprinkling the courgettes with salt helps to draw out the excess moisture so that the sauce doesn't become too runny.

1 Put the courgettes in a colander, sprinkle with salt and leave for 1 hour. Pat dry with kitchen paper.

2 Heat the oil and gently fry the onions until golden. Add the garlic, parsley and courgettes and fry until just tender, stirring frequently. Stir in the rosemary and season to taste with salt and pepper.

3 Stir in half the Parmesan and serve with the remainder.

Garlic, spinach and mushroom sauce

This is a deliciously indulgent, creamy pasta sauce. Although a whole head of garlic is used, it is roasted first, giving it a mellow, smooth flavour.

10

PREP

50

COOK

4

SERVES

feast

1 Nestle the whole garlic in a little foil and roast in a preheated oven, 200°C (400°F), Gas Mark 6, for 35–45 minutes until it is tender when pierced with a knife.

2 Meanwhile, heat the oil in a large sauce-pan and gently fry the mushrooms until they are beginning to brown. Add the spinach, cover with a lid and heat gently for a couple of minutes until the spinach has wilted.

3 Remove the roasted garlic from the oven, leave to cool slightly, then slice off the base and squeeze out the contents of each clove. Put this in a food processor with the cream cheese and nutmeg and blend until smooth.

4 Turn the garlic mixture into a saucepan, add the cream and heat gently, stirring with a wooden spoon, to make a smooth sauce. Add the mushroom and spinach mixture and heat through. Season to taste with salt and pepper.

1 small bulb of **garlic**

1 tablespoon **olive oil**

200 g (7 oz) **chestnut mushrooms**, thinly sliced

200 g (7 oz) **baby spinach leaves**

200 g (7 oz) **cream cheese**

plenty of freshly grated **nutmeg**

100 ml (3½ fl oz) **single cream**

salt and **pepper**

4 tablespoons **olive oil**

2 tablespoons flaked **almonds**

1 large **onion**, chopped

3 **garlic cloves**, crushed

½ teaspoon **ground cinnamon**

½ teaspoon crushed **dried chillies**

good pinch of **ground turmeric**

500 g (1 lb) **sweet potatoes**, cut into 1 cm (½ inch) dice

450 ml (¾ pint) **vegetable stock** (see page 21)

400 g (13 oz) can **chickpeas**, drained and rinsed

15 g (½ oz) **raisins**

salt and **pepper**

15

PREP

25

COOK

4

SERVES

sweet

Sweet potato and chickpea sauce

This recipe provides an interesting contrast between the savoury spicy potatoes and the bursts of sweetness from the raisins.

1 Heat the oil in a saucepan and fry the almonds until lightly browned. Lift out with a slotted spoon. Add the onion to the pan and gently fry for 5 minutes or until softened. Add the garlic and spices and fry for a further 1 minute. Add the sweet potatoes and fry for a further 5 minutes.

2 Add the stock and chickpeas and bring to the boil. Reduce the heat and simmer gently, covered, for about 10 minutes or until the sauce is pulpy and the sweet potatoes are tender. Use a potato masher to break them up without mashing them to a pulp.

3 Stir the raisins and almonds into the sauce, then season to taste with salt and pepper.

Curried bean sauce

20
PREP

30
COOK

4
SERVES

spicy

Curry sauce improves with keeping and can be made the day before. Serve the sauce and pasta with some side dishes such as banana slices that have been sprinkled with lemon juice, cucumber slices and mango chutney.

1 Heat the oil in a saucepan and gently fry the onion and garlic for 2–3 minutes. Stir in the curry powder, cumin, coriander, chilli powder, ginger, if using, and flour and cook for a further 1 minute.

2 Pour in the stock and lemon juice, bring to the boil, then cover, reduce the heat and simmer gently for 25 minutes. Taste and add salt if necessary

3 Add the beans to the sauce, stirring them in gently. If the sauce is too thick, thin with the reserved bean liquid.

1 tablespoon **vegetable oil**

3 **onions**, chopped

2 **garlic cloves**, crushed

3 tablespoons **curry powder**

½ teaspoon **ground cumin**

½ teaspoon **ground coriander**

½ teaspoon **chilli powder**

2 teaspoons grated fresh **root ginger** (optional)

2 tablespoons **wholemeal flour**

900 ml (1½ pints) **vegetable stock** (see page 21)

1 tablespoon **lemon juice**

2 x 400 g (13 oz) cans **red kidney beans**, drained (liquid reserved)

salt

25 g (1 oz) **dried morels** or **dried porcini**, soaked in 250 ml (8 fl oz) warm water for 20 minutes

2 tablespoons **olive oil**

25 g (1 oz) **butter**

375 g (12 oz) large **flat cap mushrooms**, chopped into 1 cm (½ inch) pieces

1 **garlic clove**, finely chopped

3 tablespoons finely chopped **parsley**

50 g (2 oz) **pine nuts**, toasted

450 ml (¾ pint) **double cream**

4 tablespoons freshly grated **Parmesan cheese**

salt and **pepper**

30
PREP

10
COOK

4

SERVES

rich

Mushroom and pine nut sauce

This selection of mushrooms combined with cream and Parmesan results in a sauce that is rich and flavoursome. The mushrooms need to be soaked in water before use in order to rehydrate them.

1 Drain the morels, reserving the water, and squeeze to extract the excess liquid. Chop into 1 cm (½ inch) pieces. Strain the soaking water and reserve.

2 Heat the olive oil and butter in a large pan. Stir-fry the morels and fresh mushrooms over a medium-high heat for 5 minutes. Stir in the garlic, parsley and the soaking water. Stir-fry until the liquid has evaporated. Season to taste with salt and pepper.

3 Add the pine nuts, cream and Parmesan and stir until heated through.

Yellow pepper sauce

20
PREP

20
COOK

4
SERVES

sweet

Yellow peppers have a sweet flavour, which partners the basil well in this recipe. Choose buffalo mozzarella and allow it to begin to melt into the pasta before tucking in.

1 Place the peppers in a saucepan with the onion, tomatoes and a pinch of salt. Cover and cook gently for about 5 minutes. Add the stock and bring to the boil, then reduce the heat and simmer for a further 15 minutes.

2 Stir in the basil and season to taste with salt and pepper. Garnish with shredded basil and serve scattered with the mozzarella.

2 large **yellow peppers**, cored, deseeded and finely chopped

½ **onion**, thinly sliced

6 **plum tomatoes**, skinned (see page 16) and chopped

250 ml (8 fl oz) **vegetable stock** (see page 21)

½ teaspoon chopped **basil**

salt and **pepper**

shredded **basil leaves**, to garnish

200 g (7 oz) **mozzarella cheese**, diced, to serve

1 tablespoon **olive oil**

1 **onion**, finely chopped

400 g (13 oz) jar **red peppers**, drained and cut into cubes

5 pieces **sun-dried tomato**, drained and thinly sliced

1–2 **garlic cloves**, crushed

400 g (13 oz) can **chopped tomatoes**

150 ml (¼ pint) **vegetable stock** (see page 21)

2 teaspoons **caster sugar**

3 tablespoons **double cream**

salt and **pepper**

basil leaves, to garnish

freshly grated **Parmesan cheese**, to serve

PREP **10**

COOK **20**

2
SERVES

simple

Creamy red pepper sauce

Combine this sauce with spaghetti, serve with a salad and you have a simple but luxuriously tasty dinner in an instant.

1 Heat the oil in a saucepan, add the onion and fry for 5 minutes, stirring occasionally, until pale golden.

2 Add the peppers, sun-dried tomatoes and the garlic. Fry for another 2 minutes, then add the tomatoes, stock, sugar and a dash of salt and pepper. Bring to the boil, then reduce the heat and simmmer for 10 minutes, stirring from time to time, then stir in the cream. Garnish with basil and serve with grated Parmesan.

Creamy spinach and nutmeg sauce

Spinach and cream are a match made in heaven. The cornflour helps to thicken the sauce, while a pinch of nutmeg adds an unusual twist.

15
PREP

20
COOK

4
SERVES

stylish

500 g (1 lb) **spinach**, tough stalks discarded

25 g (1 oz) **butter**

1 tablespoon **olive oil**

1 **onion**, finely chopped

2 **garlic cloves**, chopped

2 teaspoons **cornflour**

300 ml (½ pint) **single cream** or **double cream**

freshly grated **nutmeg**

salt and **pepper**

freshly grated **Parmesan cheese**, to serve (optional)

1 Put the spinach in a large saucepan with just the water that clings to the leaves and cook over a high heat for 3–4 minutes or until tender. Drain thoroughly, reserving the water, and set the spinach aside. Make the water up to 150 ml (¼ pint).

2 Heat the butter and oil in a large, heavy-based saucepan, add the onion, cover the pan and cook gently for 10 minutes, stirring from time to time. Stir in the garlic and cook for 1–2 more minutes.

3 Stir the cornflour into the saucepan, then add the spinach water and stir over the heat for 1–2 minutes until thickened. Add the spinach and the cream, then add a generous grating of nutmeg and season to taste with salt and pepper. Serve with grated Parmesan, if using.

500 ml (17 fl oz) **vegetable stock** (see page 21)

300 g (10 oz) **wild mushrooms**, such as chanterelles or morels, thinly sliced, pieces of stem and peel reserved

15 g (½ oz) **butter**

1 tablespoon **olive oil**

1 bunch **spring onions**, finely chopped

4 tablespoons dry **white wine**

350 ml (12 fl oz) **whipping cream** or **crème fraîche**

2 tablespoons toasted **pine nuts**

salt and **pepper**

15

PREP

25

COOK

4

SERVES

rich

Creamy chanterelle sauce

Wild mushrooms are the main ingredient in this sauce, and their intense flavour means that they can really hold their own. To give a rich, creamy finish, they are partnered with butter, oil, cream and wine – delicious!

1 Pour the stock into a saucepan and bring to the boil. Add the mushroom peelings and cook over a medium-high heat until reduced to 125 ml (4 fl oz). Strain through a sieve and discard the mushroom peelings.

2 Heat the butter and oil in a large saucepan and add the mushrooms and spring onions. Cook, stirring, until the mushrooms begin to render liquid. Add the wine and cook over a high heat until all of the liquid has nearly evaporated.

3 Add the reduced stock and cream to the mushroom mixture. Bring to the boil and reduce the sauce to half its original volume. Season to taste with salt and pepper. Add the pine nuts to the pan and toss to coat with the sauce.

Saffron sauce

5

PREP

3

COOK

2

SERVES

posh

Saffron is the world's most expensive spice, but luckily you don't need much, as it has such a pungent flavour. This simple sauce is a great everyday dish that will feel that little bit extra special.

1 Heat the butter and cream in a small saucepan, add the saffron and cook gently for a few minutes.

2 Season to taste and serve at once with grated Parmesan.

25 g (1 oz) **butter**

150 ml (¼ pint) **double cream**

½ teaspoon **saffron threads**

salt and **pepper**

75 g (3 oz) **Parmesan cheese**, freshly grated, to serve

Alfredo sauce

25 g (1 oz) **butter**

1 **onion**, chopped finely

3 **garlic cloves**, finely chopped

450 ml (¾ pint) **double cream**

¼ teaspoon grated **nutmeg**

50 g (2 oz) **Parmesan cheese**, freshly grated

salt and **pepper**

1 tablespoon chopped **parsley**, to garnish

PREP

10

COOK

5

SERVES

4

classic

A classic Italian sauce that should be served with fettuccine. It's quick and simple to prepare and the key is to use a really good quality Parmesan.

1 Melt the butter in a very large frying pan. Add the onion and garlic and fry over a high heat for 1 minute, stirring constantly.

2 Warm the cream in a saucepan. Pour it over the onion mixture and add the nutmeg. Bring the mixture to the boil and season with salt and pepper to taste.

3 Add the Parmesan and stir well. As soon as the cheese has melted, garnish with the parsley and serve.

Sorrel sauce

Sorrel is an underrated and underused ingredient. This sauce shows it off well and is excellent served with ribbon pastas.

1 Place the sorrel and stock in a saucepan, bring to the boil, then reduce the heat and simmer for 5 minutes. Cool slightly, then purée in a blender.

2 Melt the butter in a saucepan, add the flour and stir over a low heat until blended. Add the sorrel purée, stirring, then bring to the boil, reduce the heat and simmer for 4 minutes. Add the cream and season to taste with salt and pepper.

10
PREP

15
COOK

2
SERVES

herby

125 g (4 oz) **sorrel**, central stalks cut out and leaves chopped

300 ml (½ pint) **vegetable stock** (see page 21)

15 g (½ oz) **butter**

1 tablespoon **plain flour**

4 tablespoons **single cream**

salt and **pepper**

2 tablespoons **olive oil**

2 **garlic cloves**, crushed

2 x 400 g (13 oz) cans **chickpeas**, drained and rinsed, reserving 4 tablespoons liquid

2 tablespoons **tahini paste**

2 tablespoons finely chopped **parsley**, half reserved for garnish

2 tablespoons **lemon juice**, or to taste

½ pint (300 ml) **cold water**

salt and **pepper**

10

PREP

20

COOK

4

SERVES

tasty

Chickpea and tahini sauce

Tahini is made from ground sesame seeds, and it's used a lot in Middle Eastern cuisine. Try this sauce with large conchiglie pasta.

1 Heat the oil in a heavy-based saucepan, add the garlic and fry very gently until it is just beginning to change colour.

2 Add the remaining ingredients, including the reserved chickpea liquid, and bring slowly to the boil, stirring, then reduce the heat and simmer for 10 minutes.

3 Transfer the chickpea mixture to a blender and blend it to a purée (or push the mixture through a sieve). Return the purée to the rinsed-out pan and heat it through. If the sauce is a little too thick, add a few tablespoons of water until it is the right consistency for pouring over pasta. Season to taste with salt and pepper and serve garnished with the remaining parsley.

Courgette and red pesto

10

PREP

This is a quick and easy recipe that can be served warm or left to cool. It should be served with penne or other shaped pasta.

5

COOK

1 Heat 2 tablespoons of the oil in a deep frying pan. Add the garlic, lemon rind, chilli and courgettes and fry for 2–3 minutes until the courgettes are golden.

2 Add the remaining oil, the basil, red pesto and plenty of pepper. Stir over a low heat to warm through gently.

4

SERVES

easy

6 tablespoons **olive oil**

2 **garlic cloves**, sliced

1 teaspoon grated **lemon rind**

1 **dried red chilli**, deseeded and crushed

500 g (1 lb) **courgettes**, thinly sliced

1 tablespoon shredded **basil leaves**

2–3 tablespoons **red pesto**

pepper

375 g (12 oz) frozen **broad beans**

75 g (3 oz) **marinated charred artichokes**, roughly chopped

1 **garlic clove**, chopped

15 g (½ oz) **parsley**, chopped

1 tablespoon **pine nuts**

15 g (½ oz) **pecorino cheese**, freshly grated, plus extra to serve

150 ml (¼ pint) extra virgin **olive oil**

salt and **pepper**

10 PREP

5 COOK

4 SERVES

quick

Broad bean and artichoke pesto

Marinated charred artichokes are often sold in jars. If you can't find them, use canned artichoke hearts instead. Serve the sauce with penne.

1 Cook the broad beans in a pan of lightly salted, boiling water for 3 minutes. Drain and set aside, reserving 4 tablespoons of the cooking water.

2 Put the artichokes, garlic, parsley and pine nuts in a food processor and process until fairly smooth. Transfer the mixture to a bowl and stir in the pecorino and oil. Season to taste with salt and pepper.

3 Return the broad beans to the saucepan, along with the artichoke mixture and 4 tablespoons of hot water. Stir over a medium heat for a few minutes until warmed through, then season to taste. Serve with grated pecorino.

Walnut pesto genoese

Pesto sauce containing waxy potatoes and green beans is a traditional recipe from Liguria in Italy, the region around Genoa, but in this version walnuts have been used instead of pine nuts, which add a slightly bitter taste.

1 Put the crushed garlic in a food processor or blender with the olive oil and basil leaves and blend to a rough paste or use a pestle and mortar.

2 Add half of the walnuts, the Parmesan and chilli flakes and blend to a textured paste. Season to taste with salt and pepper.

3 Place the potatoes in a saucepan of boiling water and boil for 8–10 minutes or until just cooked but still firm. In a separate saucepan boil the green beans for 4–5 minutes.

4 Drain the potatoes and beans and return both to one large pan. Add the pesto sauce and toss together while still hot. Add the remaining walnuts, garnish with some extra olive oil, if liked, and serve at once with Parmesan shavings.

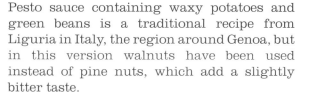

20
PREP

10
COOK

4
SERVES

hearty

3 **garlic cloves**, crushed

150 ml (¼ pint) **extra virgin olive oil**, plus extra to garnish (optional)

50 g (2 oz) **basil leaves**

125 g (4 oz) **walnuts**, roughly chopped

1 tablespoon freshly grated **Parmesan cheese**, plus shavings, to serve

pinch of **dried chilli flakes**

175 g (6 oz) small waxy **potatoes**, unpeeled, halved or quartered if large

125 g (4 oz) **green beans**, trimmed and halved

salt and **pepper**

50 g (2 oz) **coriander leaves**

2 **garlic cloves**, coarsely chopped

50 g (2 oz) roasted **cashew nuts**

1 **green chilli**, deseeded and coarsely chopped

125 ml (4 fl oz) **olive oil**

50 g (2 oz) **Parmesan cheese**, freshly grated

salt and **pepper**

10

PREP

0

COOK

4

SERVES

rich

Chilli, coriander and cashew pesto

You can use basically any type of dried or fresh pasta with this rich and creamy sauce, though long, thin pasta suits it best. Fresh pasta is ideal to use when time is very short because it cooks in minutes.

1 Process the coriander leaves with the garlic, cashew nuts, chilli and olive oil in a blender or food processor until fairly smooth and creamy.

2 Add the Parmesan and process for a few more seconds, then season to taste with salt and pepper.

Green pepper and coriander pesto

This richly flavoured sauce makes a lovely alternative to a traditional pesto (see page 24). Toss with freshly cooked pasta or use as a pasta filling. This can be kept covered and chilled for up to 3 days.

10

PREP

15

COOK

4

SERVES

tasty

100 ml (3½ fl oz) extra virgin **olive oil**

2 **green peppers**, cored, deseeded and roughly chopped

1 teaspoon **caster sugar**

75 g (3 oz) **pine nuts**

75 g (3 oz) **Parmesan cheese**, roughly sliced

2 **garlic cloves**, crushed

40 g (1½ oz) fresh **coriander leaves**

15 g (½ oz) **flat leaf parsley**

1 tablespoon **lemon juice**

salt and **pepper**

1 Heat 3 tablespoons of the oil in a frying pan and fry the peppers gently for 10–15 minutes until just beginning to colour. Stir in the sugar.

2 Tip the peppers into a food processor with the pine nuts, Parmesan, garlic, coriander and parsley. Process lightly to a very coarse paste, scraping the mixture down from the sides of the bowl if necessary.

3 Add the remaining olive oil, lemon juice and a little salt and pepper and blend again to a thick paste.

100 g (3½ oz) **sun-dried tomatoes**

75 g (3 oz) blanched **almonds**, roughly chopped

2 **garlic cloves**, roughly chopped

150 ml (¼ pint) **olive oil**

25 g (1 oz) **Parmesan cheese**, roughly sliced

salt and **pepper**

40

PREP

5

COOK

4

SERVES

tasty

Sun-dried tomato and almond pesto

You can use sun-dried tomatoes in oil instead of the dried ones in packets for this recipe. Simply drain them first (there's no need to soak them) and substitute their oil for part of the olive oil, if desired.

1 Put the tomatoes in a bowl, cover them with boiling water and leave to soak for 30 minutes until softened. Put the almonds in a dry frying pan and heat very gently, shaking the pan frequently until the almonds are beginning to turn pale golden in colour.

2 Process the almonds in a food processor until finely chopped. Thoroughly drain the tomatoes and add to the food processor with the garlic, half the oil and the Parmesan.

3 Blend the mixture until it becomes a thick paste, scraping it down from the sides of the bowl. Add the remaining oil and blend until smooth. Season to taste with salt and pepper. This sauce can be stored in the refrigerator, covered, for up to 3–4 days.

Coriander and sun-dried tomato sauce

Tomatoes and red wine combine to form a rich, hearty sauce that would work well with farfalle.

1 Heat the oil in a large frying pan. Add the onion and garlic and fry for about 3 minutes until softened but not coloured.

2 Add the red peppers and fry for a further 3 minutes. Stir in all the tomatoes and the red wine. Bring to the boil, then reduce the heat and simmer, partially covered, for 15 minutes. Season to taste with salt and pepper. Garnish with chopped coriander.

15
PREP

20
COOK

4
SERVES

hearty

2 tablespoons **olive oil**

1 **onion**, chopped

2 **garlic cloves**, crushed

2 **red peppers**, cored, deseeded and finely chopped

4 large **tomatoes**, chopped

400 g (13 oz) can **chopped tomatoes with herbs**

8 **sun-dried tomatoes** in oil, drained and sliced

150 ml (¼ pint) **red wine**

salt and **pepper**

4 tablespoons chopped fresh **coriander leaves**, to garnish

125 g (4 oz) **tofu**

2 **leeks**, chopped

3 **garlic cloves**, chopped

125 g (4 oz) frozen **peas**

8 **mushrooms**, sliced

50 g (2 oz) shelled **walnuts**, chopped

1 **bay leaf**

1 teaspoon chopped **thyme**

500 ml (17 fl oz) **milk**

1 dessertspoon **cornflour**

juice of 1 lime

2 teaspoons chopped fresh **coriander leaves**

pepper

15

PREP

15

COOK

4

SERVES

hearty

Tofu, leek and walnut sauce

The tofu helps to thicken this sauce and it also adds protein, which is important in a vegetarian diet, in the absence of meat or fish.

1 Place the tofu, leeks, garlic, peas, mushrooms, walnuts, bay leaf, thyme and milk in a large saucepan, bring to the boil, then reduce the heat and simmer for about 10 minutes.

2 Put the cornflour in a small bowl, add the lime juice and stir until smooth.

3 Take the vegetables off the heat and stir in the cornflour mixture until the sauce thickens. Stir in the coriander and black pepper to taste, then serve.

Leek and green peppercorn sauce

15

PREP

5

COOK

4

SERVES

rich

Green peppercorns are from the same plant as black peppercorns but they are picked at an earlier stage. Their flavour is less intense, which makes them ideal for using in greater quantities in sauces.

1 Heat the oil in a large frying pan and gently fry the leeks with the green peppercorns for about 3–4 minutes until the leeks are just tender.

2 Stir in the parsley and cream, then heat through, and season to taste with salt and pepper. Serve with grated Parmesan.

3 tablespoons **olive oil**

750 g (1½ lb) **leeks**, sliced lengthways and cut into matchstick strips

2 teaspoons **green peppercorns**, crushed

3 tablespoons chopped **flat leaf parsley**

300 ml (½ pint) **whipping cream**

salt and **pepper**

4 tablespoons freshly grated **Parmesan cheese**

2 teaspoons **olive oil**

1 small **onion**, finely chopped

1 small **garlic clove**, crushed

100 g (3½ oz) **carrot**, diced

250 g (8 oz) **mixed prepared vegetables**, such as red pepper, courgette, green beans, celery, mushrooms or butternut squash, diced

200 g (7 oz) can **plum tomatoes**

large pinch of **dried marjoram** or **dried oregano**

freshly grated **Parmesan cheese**, to serve

20
PREP

15
COOK

2
SERVES

tasty

Smooth vegetable sauce

Vary the vegetables for this recipe according to what you have in the fridge. Flavour the sauce with a few sprigs of fresh herbs, such as basil or marjoram, or a mixture of herbs.

1 Heat the oil in a large saucepan. Add the onion and fry for about 4–5 minutes, stirring occasionally, until lightly browned. Add the garlic and vegetables and fry for another 2 minutes.

2 Stir in the tomatoes with their juice, and the herbs. Bring to the boil, breaking up the tomatoes with a spoon. Reduce the heat and simmer the sauce uncovered for 5 minutes, stirring occasionally.

3 Purée the tomato mixture in a blender or processor until smooth, then return to the saucepan. Season to taste with salt and pepper, then reheat if necessary. Serve with grated Parmesan.

Calaloo sauce

5
PREP

Calaloo is Caribbean spinach, available from West Indian grocers, usually in cans. If you can't find it, use fresh spinach instead.

10
COOK

1 Heat the olive oil in a medium saucepan and fry the shallots until golden. Add the calaloo and stir until hot.

2 Over a low heat, add the coconut cream, a little at a time, then the bouillon powder, garlic and basil. Stirring constantly, add the wine. Season to taste with salt and pepper, then garnish with basil.

2
SERVES

exotic

1 tablespoon **olive oil**

2 **shallots**, chopped

275 g (9 oz) can **calaloo**, drained, or 250 g (8 oz) **spinach**, chopped

6 tablespoons **coconut cream**

2 teaspoons **bouillon powder**

1 **garlic clove**, crushed

4 **basil leaves**, chopped, plus whole leaves to garnish

4 tablespoons dry **white wine**, or half and half **lemon juice** and **water**

salt and **pepper**

1 small **onion**, finely chopped

185 g (6½ oz) can **pimentos**, drained and thinly sliced

400 g (13 oz) can **chopped tomatoes with herbs**

425 g (14 oz) can **mixed bean salad**, drained

1 teaspoon **tomato purée**

2 tablespoons chopped **parsley**

salt and **pepper**

sprigs of **chervil**, to garnish

5

PREP

25

COOK

4

SERVES

hearty

Mixed bean sauce

Mixed bean salad is a combination of green, red kidney, black eye, borlotti and cannellini beans with chickpeas, sweetcorn and red peppers. It makes a wonderful base for a hearty pasta sauce.

1 Heat a heavy-based frying pan and dry-fry the onion for 3–6 minutes, stirring constantly.

2 Add the pimentos and fry for another 1–2 minutes. Add the tomatoes with their juice, the beans and tomato purée. Bring to the boil, stir well, then reduce the heat and simmer for about 15 minutes.

3 Stir half of the parsley into the bean sauce. Season to taste with salt and pepper and serve garnished with the remaining parsley and chervil.

Italian vegetable sauce

This is a great sauce to make when summer vegetables are plentiful. Serve as a topping to plain pasta or use for layering in lasagne and other baked pasta dishes.

1 Heat the oil in a large saucepan, add the onion, peppers, celery and courgette and cook for about 2 minutes, stirring, until almost tender.

2 Stir in the tomatoes, spinach, stock and sugar. Bring to the boil, then reduce the heat and simmer for 10 minutes until the sauce has reduced and thickened. Season to taste with salt and pepper.

15 PREP

15 COOK

4 SERVES

hearty

1 tablespoon **olive oil**

1 **onion**, finely chopped

1 **red pepper**, cored, deseeded and finely chopped

1 **yellow pepper**, cored, deseeded and finely chopped

2 **celery sticks**, finely chopped

1 **courgette**, finely chopped

4 **tomatoes**, skinned (see page 16), deseeded and chopped

250 g (8 oz) **spinach**, tough stalks discarded, chopped

150 ml (¼ pint) **vegetable stock** (see page 21)

1 teaspoon **caster sugar**

salt and **pepper**

2 tablespoons **olive oil**

1 **onion**, finely chopped

4 **garlic cloves**, crushed

2 **red peppers**, cored, deseeded and finely sliced

1 tablespoon chopped **basil**

1 tablespoon chopped **oregano**

1 tablespoon chopped **parsley**

300 ml (½ pint) **double cream**

salt and **pepper**

1 tablespoon torn **mixed herbs**, to garnish

shavings of **Parmesan cheese**, to serve (optional)

15

PREP

8

COOK

4

SERVES

herby

Herb and garlic sauce

Nothing compares to the flavour of freshly chopped herbs and this sauce takes full advantage of them. The freshness of parsley, the distinct Italian flavour and aroma of basil and the intense taste of oregano all work fantastically well together.

1 Heat the olive oil in a large frying pan. Add the onion, garlic and red peppers, and fry the mixture over a moderate heat for about 3–5 minutes until the onion is softened but not browned.

2 Sprinkle over the chopped herbs, stir in the cream, bring to the boil, then reduce the heat and simmer for about 1 minute more. Season to taste with salt and pepper, then garnish with torn herbs and serve with Parmesan shavings, if using.

Toasted almond and parsley pesto

Pesto is a classic Italian sauce, usually made from pine nuts and basil. Here, for a change, it is made from almonds and parsley.

1 Spread the almonds on a baking sheet and place it under a preheated grill for 2–3 minutes, turning the almonds often until they are toasted and golden. (You may have to break one open to see.)

2 Place half of the toasted almonds in a blender or food processor with the garlic, Parmesan, parsley, olive oil, ricotta and salt and pepper and blend until smooth, scraping down the sides of the bowl if necessary. Roughly chop the remaining almonds and stir into the pesto.

15
PREP

3
COOK

4
SERVES

nutty

125 g (4 oz) unblanched whole **almonds**

1 **garlic clove**, crushed

2 tablespoons freshly grated **Parmesan cheese**

50 g (2 oz) **parsley**, roughly chopped

200 ml (7 fl oz) extra virgin **olive oil**

2 tablespoons **ricotta cheese**

salt and **pepper**

1½ tablespoons **sunflower oil**

1 **onion**, sliced

625 g (1¼ lb) large flat **mushrooms**, sliced

1–2 teaspoons fresh **green peppercorns** in brine, drained

1 tablespoon **soy sauce**

2 tablespoons **double cream** or **whipping cream**

2 tablespoons **pine nuts**

salt

1 tablespoon chopped **parsley**, to garnish

25
PREP

30
COOK

4
SERVES

nutty

Mushroom and peppercorn sauce

Pine nuts, the main ingredient in pesto, are used whole here. Toasting them first helps to draw out the flavours and gives them a more nutty taste. Serve this sauce with fusilli or other dried pasta shapes.

1 Heat 1 tablespoon of the sunflower oil in a large saucepan. Add the onion and fry for about 5 minutes. Add the mushrooms and cook for a further few minutes until they have cooked down a little.

2 Add the green peppercorns, soy sauce, 3 tablespoons water and a little salt. Bring to the boil, cover the saucepan, then reduce the heat and simmer gently for 15 minutes. Remove the lid and cook quickly for 3–4 minutes to reduce some of the liquid.

3 Pour the mushroom mixture into a food processor or blender and process for just a few seconds (the mushrooms should retain some texture). Return to the rinsed pan and stir in the cream.

4 Heat the remaining oil in a saucepan and fry the pine nuts for 30 seconds until golden-brown. Drain on kitchen paper and set aside.

5 Reheat the mushroom sauce without boiling and serve garnished with the browned pine nuts and chopped parsley.

Asparagus and mushroom sauce

Try to save this recipe for when asparagus is in season. To separate the spears from the woody stalks, simply bend each one gently and it will give at the natural place. Serve with fresh tagliatelle.

1 Melt the butter in a large frying pan and add the asparagus, mushrooms and ginger. Mix gently and allow the vegetables to cook slowly, without browning, for 5–8 minutes.

2 Add the tarragon and cream or crème fraîche to the pan. Season to taste with salt and pepper. Stir gently, bring to the boil, then reduce the heat and simmer for 5 minutes. Garnish with a few strips of lemon rind and parsley sprigs, if using.

10
PREP

15
COOK

4
SERVES

fresh

25 g (1 oz) **butter**

250 g (8 oz) fresh **asparagus** spears, cut into 2.5 cm (1 inch) lengths, blanched

125 g (4 oz) **chestnut mushrooms**, sliced

2.5 cm (1 inch) piece of fresh **root ginger**, peeled and grated

1 tablespoon chopped **tarragon**

250 ml (8 fl oz) **double cream** or **crème fraîche**

salt and **pepper**

TO GARNISH:

strips of **lemon** rind

parsley sprigs (optional)

8 tablespoons **olive oil**

1 large **aubergine**, cut into 1 cm (½ inch) cubes

2 **garlic cloves**, finely chopped

1 **chilli**, deseeded and finely chopped

2 x 400 g (13 oz) cans **chopped tomatoes**

salt and **pepper**

3 tablespoons chopped **flat leaf parsley**

freshly grated **Parmesan cheese**, to serve

15
PREP

40
COOK

4
SERVES

tasty

Aubergine, tomato and chilli sauce

This sauce requires a lengthy simmering period so that it can reduce down and the flavours will be more concentrated. Try serving with fusilli lunghi or fettuccine.

1 Heat the oil in a large saucepan and gently fry the aubergine for about 5 minutes. Stir in the garlic and chilli and fry until the garlic begins to colour.

2 Stir in the tomatoes and the parsley. Bring to the boil, then reduce the heat and simmer for about 30 minutes. Season to taste with salt and pepper, then serve sprinkled with grated Parmesan.

Mediterranean vegetable sauce

This is one of those great sauces that you can easily adapt when you want to try something new. So chuck in some canned beans, pitted olives or walnuts – a little of whatever you like really!

1 Put all the ingredients in a saucepan and bring to the boil. Then reduce the heat and simmer, uncovered, for 15 minutes.

2 Pour the sauce into a blender or food processor and blend until smooth. Serve with grated Parmesan.

10
PREP

15
COOK

4
SERVES

rich

400 g (13 oz) can **chopped tomatoes**

1 **onion**, chopped

1 **garlic clove**, crushed

2 tablespoons chopped **basil**

1 teaspoon **dried rosemary**

1 glass of **red wine**

freshly grated **Parmesan cheese**, to serve

3 tablespoons **olive oil**

2 **onions**, chopped

2 **garlic cloves**, crushed

500 g (1 lb) **plum tomatoes**, skinned (see page 16) and chopped

2 tablespoons **tomato purée**

1 teaspoon **caster sugar**

125 ml (4 fl oz) dry **white wine**

a few ripe **olives**, pitted and quartered

2–3 tablespoons torn **basil leaves**

salt and **pepper**

50 g (2 oz) **Parmesan cheese**, shaved, to serve

10

PREP

20

COOK

4

SERVES

classic

Sugo di pomodoro

Plum tomatoes and olives make a delicious, rich sauce. Garlic, basil and Parmesan are added for a real low-down on classic Italian ingredients. As always, the success of the sauce will be entirely down to the quality of the ingredients.

1 Heat the olive oil in a large frying pan. Add the onions and garlic and sauté gently over a low heat until they are tender and lightly coloured.

2 Add the tomatoes and the tomato purée together with the sugar and white wine, stirring well. Cook over a low heat until the mixture is quite thick and reduced. Stir in the olives and basil leaves and season to taste with salt and plenty of pepper. Serve with Parmesan shavings.

Lentil and vegetable bolognese

This tasty meat-free version of the classic Bolognese sauce is sure to please vegetarians and non-vegetarians alike!

1 Put the lentils into a saucepan, add plenty of cold water to cover and bring to the boil. Reduce the heat and simmer, uncovered, for 30 minutes or until tender. Drain and reserve.

2 Meanwhile, heat the oil in a saucepan, add the onion, garlic and carrots and fry for 4–5 minutes, stirring occasionally, until lightly browned. Add the courgettes and mushrooms and cook for 2 minutes. Stir in the tomatoes, stock, tomato purée and marjoram.

3 Bring to the boil, cover and simmer for 5 minutes, stirring occasionally. Season to taste with salt and pepper. Stir in the drained lentils and serve with grated Parmesan.

15
PREP

30
COOK

4
SERVES

hearty

75 g (3 oz) **puy lentils**, rinsed

1 tablespoon **olive oil**

1 **onion**, finely chopped

1 **garlic clove**, crushed

2 small **carrots**, diced

2 small **courgettes**, diced

50 g (2 oz) **button mushrooms**, sliced

400 g (13 oz) can **chopped tomatoes**

150 ml (¼ pint) **vegetable stock** (see page 21)

2 tablespoons **tomato purée**

3 tablespoons chopped **fresh marjoram** or ¾ teaspoon **dried marjoram**

salt and **pepper**

freshly grated **Parmesan cheese**, to serve

3 tablespoons **olive oil**

1 kg (2 lb) **plum tomatoes**, skinned (see page 16) and chopped

4 **garlic cloves**, finely chopped

½ teaspoon **dried oregano**

1 tablespoon chopped **parsley**

salt and **pepper**

freshly grated **Parmesan cheese**, to serve

15

PREP

25

COOK

4–6

SERVES

Tomato and garlic sauce

Another simple dish using basic ingredients that are readily available. Serve with linguine or spaghetti.

1 Heat the oil in a frying pan and gently fry the tomatoes and garlic over a medium-high heat for 20 minutes until thickened.

2 Add the oregano, the parsley and the salt and pepper to taste, and cook for a few minutes more.

Tomato and chilli sauce

10
PREP

15
COOK

Crushed chillies add a fiery kick to a pasta sauce and it's easy to add as little or as much as you like, depending on taste.

4
SERVES

1 Heat the oil in a saucepan, add the onion and garlic, and sauté until soft but not browned. Add the chillies and tomatoes.

2 Over low heat, add the sugar and vinegar. Mix gently, bring to the boil, then reduce the heat and simmer for 10 minutes, then season to taste with salt and pepper.

3 Stir the parsley into the sauce and serve with grated Parmesan.

spicy

3 tablespoons **olive oil**

1 **onion**, chopped

2 **garlic cloves**, chopped

2 pinches of crushed **dried chillies**, or to taste

10 ripe **plum tomatoes**, skinned (see page 16), deseeded and cut into strips

1 teaspoon **caster sugar**

1 teaspoon **vinegar**

handful of **flat leaf parsley**, chopped

salt and **pepper**

75 g (3 oz) **Parmesan cheese**, freshly grated, to serve

fish and seafood

600 ml (1 pint) **milk**

1 **carrot**

1 **onion**, studded with
2 **cloves**

1 **celery stick**

50 g (2 oz) **butter**

175 g (6 oz) **mushrooms**,
sliced

75 g (3 oz) **plain flour**

300 ml (½ pint) **chicken
stock** (see page 19)

2 tablespoons **lemon
juice**

50 g (2 oz) can **anchovy
fillets** in oil, drained and
chopped

40 g (1½ oz) **Cheddar
cheese**, grated

salt and **pepper**

25

PREP

10

COOK

6

SERVES

fresh

Mushroom, lemon and anchovy sauce

Anchovies have a wonderfully rich, salty flavour. They will begin to dissolve in the sauce, so you will be left with the essence of the fish throughout the finished dish.

1 Put the milk, carrot, onion and celery in a saucepan and bring to the boil. Remove from the heat and leave to infuse for 15 minutes, then strain.

2 Melt the butter in a frying pan and sauté the mushrooms for 3–4 minutes, before adding the flour. Cook for 2 minutes before stirring in the stock, lemon juice and infused milk. Bring to the boil, stirring, then reduce the heat and simmer for 3–4 minutes.

3 Stir the anchovies into the sauce together with the grated cheese. Season well with salt and pepper and gently reheat.

Aubergine, pepper and olive sauce

This chunky, flavoursome sauce is perfect partnered with spaghetti or linguine. The red wine will add a rich finish – choose a hearty Italian red for maximum impact.

1 Heat the oil in a large saucepan and gently fry the onion for about 3 minutes. Add the tomatoes, tomato purée, red wine, aubergine, peppers, anchovy fillets and garlic.

2 Bring to the boil, then reduce the heat and simmer gently for 20 minutes. Add the olives and season to taste with salt and pepper.

20
PREP

25
COOK

4
SERVES

gutsy

4 tablespoons **olive oil**

1 **onion**, finely chopped

400 g (13 oz) can **chopped tomatoes**

2 tablespoons **tomato purée**

150 ml (¼ pint) **red wine**

1 large **aubergine**, chopped

1 large **red pepper**, cored, deseeded and finely diced

1 large **green pepper**, cored, deseeded and finely diced

8 **anchovy fillets** in oil, drained and chopped

1 **garlic clove**, crushed

75 g (3 oz) pitted **black olives**

salt and **pepper**

100 g (3½ oz) pitted **black olives**

4 tablespoons **capers**, drained and rinsed

50 g (2 oz) **sun-dried tomatoes** in oil, drained

6 **anchovy fillets** in oil, drained

1 teaspoon **fennel seeds**, lightly crushed

small handful of **flat leaf parsley**, roughly chopped

small handful of **basil**, roughly chopped

150 ml (¼ pint) **olive oil**

salt and **pepper**

freshly grated **Parmesan cheese**, to serve (optional)

15
PREP

0
COOK

4
SERVES

simple

Olive and caper tapenade

This richly flavoured paste is transformed into a delicious sauce when stirred into freshly cooked pasta. It is a great recipe to make ahead and store in the refrigerator for an easy supper dish. Any leftovers make a good topping for crostini.

1 Put the olives, capers, tomatoes, anchovy fillets and fennel seeds into a food processor or blender and blend to a paste, scraping down the mixture from the sides of the bowl if necessary.

2 Add the parsley, basil, oil and a little salt and pepper and blend briefly until the herbs are finely chopped and all the ingredients are blended. Serve with grated Parmesan, if using.

Hot chilli tapenade

15
PREP

2
COOK

4
SERVES

spicy

This is a variation on a traditional tapenade, with the addition of hot chilli and spices, coarsely blended to make a textured pasta sauce. You can heat it gently in a small pan for a couple of minutes before tossing it with the pasta.

1 Gently heat the cumin seeds and the coriander seeds in a small, dry, frying pan until they start to toast.

2 Tip the seeds into a food processor and add the olives, capers, anchovy fillets and their oil, the garlic, parsley and chillies.

3 Blend lightly, until the ingredients start to mix together. Add the oil and blend briefly to a chunky paste.

1 teaspoon crushed **cumin seeds**

1 teaspoon crushed **coriander seeds**

150 g (5 oz) pitted **black olives**

25 g (1 oz) **capers**, drained and rinsed

50 g (2 oz) can **anchovy fillets** in oil

1 **garlic clove**, chopped

small handful of **flat leaf parsley**

15 g (½ oz) **red jalapeño chillies** in sweet vinegar, drained

125 ml (4 fl oz) **olive oil**

1 **yellow pepper**

1 **red pepper**

5 **anchovy fillets** in oil, drained

2 tablespoons **milk**

250 ml (8 fl oz) **vegetable stock** (see page 21)

2 **garlic cloves**

125 ml (4 fl oz) **sunflower oil**

3 tablespoons dry **white wine**

1 tablespoon **tomato purée**

salt and **pepper**

1 tablespoon chopped **parsley**, to garnish

25
PREP

50
COOK

4
SERVES

feast

Roasted pepper and anchovy sauce

The anchovies are soaked in milk to reduce their salty flavour, which would otherwise overpower this subtle sauce. Serve with small penne pasta.

1 Place the peppers on an oiled baking tray. Cook in a preheated oven, 220°C (425°F), Gas Mark 7, turning occasionally, until the skins are blackened and blistered. Remove from the oven and carefully peel off the skins. Remove and discard the stems and seeds, collecting any juices in a bowl. Cut the peppers into 25 x 5 mm (1 x ¼ inch) strips.

2 Meanwhile, soak the anchovies in the milk for 15 minutes to reduce the saltiness. Drain the anchovies, chop and set aside. Heat the stock in a saucepan.

3 Put the garlic and drained anchovies through a mincer or use a food processor. Heat the oil in a large pan, add the anchovy and garlic mixture and cook over a low heat until softened. Add the strips of pepper, stir and moisten with the reserved pepper juices.

4 Season lightly, pour in the wine and allow it to evaporate slowly, then add the tomato purée diluted with the hot stock. Bring to the boil, then reduce the heat and simmer for 10 minutes. Garnish with parsley.

Anchovy and oregano sauce

8

PREP

This is a very quick and simple recipe that uses anchovies as the main ingredient. The strong flavour of oregano adds another dimension to the sauce, while the Parmesan cheese provides a creamy topping.

15

COOK

1 Heat the oil in a small saucepan, add the garlic and fry gently for about 5 minutes until golden.

2 Reduce the heat to very low, stir in the anchovies and cook gently for 10 minutes until they have completely disintegrated.

3 Stir in the oregano and pepper to taste. Garnish with parsley and serve at once with grated Parmesan.

2

SERVES

quick

1 tablespoon **olive oil**

2 **garlic cloves**, finely chopped

50 g (2 oz) can **anchovy fillets** in oil, drained and chopped

2 teaspoons **oregano**, finely chopped

pepper

3 tablespoons chopped **parsley**, to garnish

freshly grated **Parmesan cheese**, to serve

25 g (1 oz) **butter**

6 **anchovy fillets** in oil, drained and chopped

1 tablespoon **tomato purée**

1 tablespoon **olive paste**

6 pitted **black olives**, chopped

pepper

handful of **basil leaves**, torn, to garnish

freshly grated **Parmesan cheese**, to serve

10

PREP

5

COOK

2

SERVES

tasty

Anchovy and olive sauce

The combination of olives and anchovies in this sauce is fantastic. Both ingredients have a salty flavour so they complement each other, without losing their individuality. This recipe would work well with fusilli pasta.

1 Melt the butter in a large saucepan. Add the anchovy fillets, tomato purée, olive paste and olives. Stir over the heat until the mixture sizzles.

2 Season the sauce well with pepper, garnish with basil and serve with grated Parmesan.

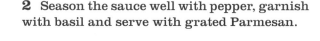

Clam and tomato sauce

Fresh clams cooked in a tomato sauce are a variation on the classic Vongole Sauce (see page 42). You may have to cook this sauce on the spur of the moment as fresh clams, for many of us, are not very widely available.

1 Scrub the clams, discarding any damaged ones or open ones that do not close when tapped with a knife.

2 Heat the oil in a large, heavy-based saucepan. Add the garlic and chillies and fry gently for 1 minute. Add the wine and let it bubble for 2 minutes, then add the tomatoes and sugar. Bring the sauce to the boil and cook for 8–10 minutes until it is thickened and pulpy, breaking up the tomatoes with a wooden spoon.

3 Tip the clams into the pan, cover with a lid and cook for 3–4 minutes until the clams have opened. Using a slotted spoon, lift about two-thirds of the clams out of the pan and remove them from their shells, discarding any shells that have not opened. Return the clams to the pan with the parsley, lemon rind and juice and salt and pepper to taste. Heat through for 2 minutes.

20
PREP

20
COOK

4
SERVES

stylish

1 kg (2 lb) small fresh **clams**

4 tablespoons **olive oil**

3 **garlic cloves**, crushed

¼ teaspoon crushed **dried chillies**

150 ml (¼ pint) dry **white wine**

2 x 400 g (13 oz) cans **plum tomatoes**

1 teaspoon **caster sugar**

small handful of **flat leaf parsley**, chopped

finely grated **rind and juice of ½ lemon**

salt and **pepper**

2 kg (4 lb) fresh **mussels**

3 tablespoons **olive oil**

1 **onion**, finely chopped

2 **garlic cloves**, sliced

750 g (1½ lb) **tomatoes**, skinned (see page 16) and chopped

salt and **pepper**

flat leaf parsley, to garnish

45

PREP

45

COOK

3

SERVES

rustic

Mussel and tomato sauce

This sauce is best served with spaghetti but you could also try linguine. There are just a few simple ingredients, which are really there to add a touch of flavour to the mussels. This is typical of Italian cooking.

1 First prepare the mussels. Put them into a bowl covered with cold water. Discard any that are open. Scrub the mussels to remove any barnacles and remove the beards. Soak in fresh cold water until ready to cook.

2 Heat the olive oil in a saucepan. Add the onion and sauté for 5 minutes until soft. Stir in the garlic, then the tomatoes. Boil, then reduce the heat and simmer for 30 minutes until the tomatoes have reduced to a pulp.

3 Meanwhile, put the mussels in a large saucepan with 150 ml (¼ pint) water. Heat briskly, shaking the pan occasionally, for 5–6 minutes or until the shells open. Discard any mussels that do not open.

4 Remove the mussels from the heat and drain the water. Reserve a few of the mussels in their shells for the garnish; remove the rest from their shells and set aside.

5 Season with salt and pepper to taste, add the shelled mussels and heat through, stirring all the time. Garnish with the reserved mussels and flat leaf parsley.

Mussel and saffron cream sauce

Luxurious saffron works really well with cream and this would make a great dinner party dish as it is subtle yet unusual. Shallots have a sweeter flavour than onions, so are perfect for this particular recipe.

45

PREP

25

COOK

4

SERVES

posh

1 Soak the saffron in 2 tablespoons of hot water for about 5 minutes.

2 Put the mussels in a large saucepan with the white wine and the shallots. Heat briskly, shaking the pan occasionally, for about 5–6 minutes or until the shells open. Discard any mussels that do not open. Leave to stand for 5 minutes.

3 Strain the liquid through a coffee filter and pour into a clean pan. Boil until reduced to about 150 ml (¼ pint). Shell the mussels and keep warm.

4 Add the cream and the saffron, with its soaking water, to the mussel liquid. Bring to the boil, then reduce the heat and simmer for about 5 minutes until thickened. Season to taste with salt and pepper.

large pinch of **saffron** threads

2 litres (3½ pints) **mussels**, scrubbed and bearded (see page 176)

175 ml (6 fl oz) dry **white wine**

2 **shallots**, finely chopped

150 ml (¼ pint) **double cream**

salt and **pepper**

Lobster sauce

3 small live **lobsters** or **lobster tails**, weighing about 400 g (13 oz) each

3 tablespoons **olive oil**

2–3 **garlic cloves**, chopped

large pinch of crushed **dried chillies**

1 glass dry **white wine**

1 tablespoon chopped **parsley**, plus extra to garnish

salt and **pepper**

10

PREP

20

COOK

6

SERVES

simple

If you cannot find any small lobsters, the equivalent weight in Dublin Bay prawns will do just as well. Eat the lobster from the shells with your fingers – sucking the shells is part of the fun.

1 Bring a large pan of salted water to the boil, drop in 1 lobster, then reduce the heat and simmer for 12 minutes. Leave to cool, then remove the flesh from the shells.

2 Split the other 2 lobsters in half with a sharp knife lengthways, remove and discard the stomach sacs, then chop them into large pieces, legs, head and all.

3 Heat the oil in a frying pan, add the garlic, chillies and chopped lobster. Sauté for a couple of minutes, then add the wine. Bring to the boil, then add the boiled lobster meat, stir in the parsley and heat through. Season to taste with salt and pepper and garnish with the extra parsley.

Creamy crab and artichoke sauce

The unusual combination of artichoke hearts and crab, served in a rich creamy sauce, makes a lovely dish for special occasions. Serve with fresh linguine verde.

10
PREP

10
COOK

4
SERVES

rich

750 ml (1¼ pints) **whipping cream**

50 g (2 oz) **unsalted butter**, at room temperature

125 g (4 oz) canned **artichoke hearts**, drained and halved

3 **spring onions**, cut into 2.5 cm (1 inch) lengths

50 g (2 oz) **Parmesan cheese**, freshly grated

250 g (8 oz) cooked **crab meat**

salt and **pepper**

flat leaf parsley, to garnish

1 Pour the cream into a saucepan and boil until reduced to 350 ml (12 fl oz). Add a little of the butter, then add the artichoke hearts and spring onions and sauté for 2–3 minutes. Add half of the Parmesan and the crab meat and cook until just heated through.

2 Season with salt and pepper to taste, garnish with parsley and serve with the remaining Parmesan.

1 teaspoon **olive oil**

4 **garlic cloves**, finely sliced

375 ml (13 fl oz) can low-fat **evaporated milk**

finely grated **rind of 2 lemons**

4 teaspoons **French mustard**

1 teaspoon **cornflour**

50 ml (2 fl oz) **water**

200 g (7 oz) can **crab meat**, flaked

pepper

Crab and lemon sauce

PREP

COOK

SERVES

If you're feeling adventurous, you could prepare your own crab meat from fresh crabs. It takes a little practice but the results are well worth the effort. Try this sauce with angel hair pasta.

1 Heat the oil in a saucepan. Add the garlic and cook over a low heat for about 2 minutes or until the garlic is golden. Remove the garlic from the pan and set aside.

2 Add the evaporated milk, lemon rind and mustard to the pan. Bring slowly to the boil, then reduce the heat and simmer for about 2 minutes.

3 Place the cornflour in a small bowl and stir in the water to form a smooth paste. Stir the cornflour paste into the milk mixture. Stir constantly over a medium heat until the mixture boils and thickens.

4 Add the crab meat and cooked garlic and season to taste with black pepper.

Crab and chilli sauce

PREP 5

Sweet crab meat and shallots are partnered with hot chillies and cream for a decadent pasta sauce that is rich and thick. Serve with tagliatelle or spaghetti.

COOK 10

1 Heat the olive oil in a saucepan, add the shallots and sauté gently until soft, but do not brown.

2 Add the crab meat, chillies, lemon rind and juice and season with salt and pepper to taste.

3 Add the cream to the crab mixture and bring to the boil, then add the chives. Serve with a bowl of grated Parmesan.

SERVES 4

feast

2 tablespoons **olive oil**

2 **shallots**, chopped

200 g (7 oz) **crab meat**

1–2 pinches crushed **dried chillies**

grated **rind and juice of 1 lemon**

4 tablespoons **double cream**

handful of **chives**, snipped

salt and **pepper**

75 g (3 oz) **Parmesan cheese**, freshly grated, to serve

8 tablespoons **olive oil**

2 **garlic cloves**, finely chopped

2 **fennel bulbs**, trimmed and very thinly sliced lengthways

500 g (1 lb) **scallops**, thinly sliced

4 tablespoons chopped **flat leaf parsley**

salt and **pepper**

TO SERVE:

4 tablespoons freshly grated **Parmesan cheese**

4 tablespoons **toasted breadcrumbs**

10
PREP

10
COOK

4
SERVES

filling

Scallop and fennel sauce

Scallops need just the minimum amount of cooking – too much and they will become chewy and rubbery. They work well in pasta sauces as they will absorb the other flavours and produce a sauce with bulk and texture.

1 Heat the oil and gently fry the garlic for a few seconds until just pale golden. Stir in the fennel, cover and cook gently for 5 minutes until just tender.

2 Add the scallops and parsley and stir-fry over a medium-high heat for 3–5 minutes. Season to taste with salt and pepper and serve with grated Parmesan and breadcrumbs.

Crayfish sauce with tarragon

Curly pink crayfish tails, cooked and brined, are often available from the fishmonger or in little tubs from the supermarket.

10

PREP

25

COOK

2

SERVES

herby

300 ml (½ pint) **fish stock** (see page 18)

½ glass of **white wine**

1 **bay leaf**

several sprigs of **thyme**

15 g (½ oz) **butter**

1 tablespoon **plain flour**

150 ml (¼ pint) **double cream**

1 tablespoon **tomato purée**

1 tablespoon chopped **tarragon**

1 tablespoon **brandy** (optional)

150 g (5 oz) **crayfish tails**, thoroughly rinsed and drained

salt and **pepper**

1 Put the stock, white wine and herbs in a saucepan and bring to the boil. Boil until reduced to about 200 ml (7 fl oz). This will take 10–15 minutes.

2 Melt the butter in a separate saucepan. Add the flour and cook for 1 minute to make a golden paste. Gradually blend in the stock, discarding the herbs. Cook gently, stirring, until thickened and smooth.

3 Stir in the cream, tomato purée, tarragon and brandy, if using, and bring slowly to the boil, then reduce the heat and simmer.

4 Stir in the crayfish tails and heat through gently for 2 minutes. Season to taste with salt and pepper and serve.

300 g (10 oz) small **squid**, rinsed and thinly sliced, tentacles used too if present

3 tablespoons **olive oil**

2 **garlic cloves**, crushed

400 g (13 oz) can **chopped tomatoes**

2 tablespoons **sun-dried tomato paste**

4 tablespoons chopped **parsley**

25 g (1 oz) **gherkins**, finely chopped

2 tablespoons **capers** in brine, drained, rinsed and chopped

salt and **pepper**

10

PREP

10

COOK

2–3

SERVES

fresh

Squid and tomato tartare sauce

This colourful, fresh and tangy sauce has a distinct Mediterranean flavour and is perfect with almost any pasta. It looks stunning with squid ink pasta.

1 Pat the squid dry on kitchen paper.

2 Heat the oil in a large frying pan and gently fry the squid for 2–3 minutes or until puffed into rings. Add the garlic and fry gently for another minute.

3 Add the remaining ingredients to the frying pan. Bring to the boil, then reduce the heat and simmer gently for 5 minutes or until the sauce is thickened and heated through. Season to taste with salt and pepper and serve.

Prawn and vodka sauce

10

PREP

Despite sounding quite unusual, vodka is used in a number of pasta sauce recipes. Here, it combines with white wine, herbs and prawns for a rustic sauce that is best served with spaghetti.

25

COOK

1 Heat half the oil in a frying pan. Add the onion and cook it gently for about 5 minutes, stirring frequently, until softened.

2 Add the tomatoes and garlic and stir the tomatoes well to break them up, pressing them against the side of the pan if necessary. Add the wine, if using, the tomato purée, rosemary and basil leaves.

3 Bring to the boil, then reduce the heat and simmer, uncovered, for about 15 minutes, stirring until the sauce is reduced to a thick purée. Remove the pan from the heat. Season to taste with salt and pepper.

4 Meanwhile, heat the remaining oil in a frying pan. Add the butter and heat until it is sizzling. Add the prawns and mushrooms, stirring well. Pour in the vodka, increase the heat and cook, stirring constantly, until all the liquid has evaporated.

5 Add the tomato sauce and cream and stir until well blended and heated. Garnish with a few unpeeled prawns and basil leaves.

4

SERVES

rustic

3 tablespoons **olive oil**

1 small **onion**, finely chopped

250 g (8 oz) can **plum tomatoes**

1 **garlic clove**, crushed

3 tablespoons dry **white wine** (optional)

1 teaspoon **tomato purée**

a few sprigs of **rosemary** and **basil leaves**

15 g (½ oz) **butter**

250 g (8 oz) peeled **prawns**, thawed and dried if frozen

300 g (10 oz) can whole **button mushrooms**, drained

4 tablespoons **vodka**

75 ml (3 fl oz) **double cream**

salt and **pepper**

TO GARNISH:

cooked unpeeled **prawns**

basil leaves

75 ml (3 fl oz) **olive oil**

1 large **onion**, finely chopped

2 **garlic cloves**, crushed

2 x 400 g (13 oz) cans **chopped tomatoes**

150 ml (¼ pint) dry **white wine**

pinch of **brown sugar**

½ teaspoon **dried thyme**

500 g (1 lb) peeled **prawns**

125 g (4 oz) cooked or canned shelled **mussels**

salt and **pepper**

chopped **parsley**, to garnish

10

PREP

30

COOK

6

SERVES

feast

Prawn and mussel sauce

This is a real seafood feast, with prawns and mussels being added at the last minute to a wonderfully rich, reduced tomato sauce. This would be good with macaroni.

1 Heat the oil in a large saucepan. Add the onion and garlic and cook until golden. Add the tomatoes and their juice, wine, sugar and thyme. Bring to the boil, then reduce the heat and simmer gently for 15–20 minutes. Season to taste with salt and pepper.

2 Stir in the prawns and mussels and cook for a further 3 minutes, stirring occasionally. Garnish with chopped parsley.

Prawn and brandy sauce

10 PREP

5 COOK

2 SERVES

simple

25 g (1 oz) **butter**

4 **plum tomatoes**, skinned (see page 16) and chopped

2 tablespoons **brandy**

200 g (7 oz) cooked peeled **prawns**, thawed if frozen

3 tablespoons **double cream**

1 tablespoon chopped **tarragon**

salt and **pepper**

Small prawns are often sweeter than the big tiger prawns, and that's exactly what you want in this dish. Frozen ones are fine. Make sure you boil off the brandy properly to remove its slightly 'raw' taste before adding the prawns and herbs.

1 Heat the butter in a frying pan and fry the tomatoes for 2–3 minutes until they have softened. Pour in the brandy, turn up the heat to high and cook for 2 minutes.

2 Add the prawns, cream and tarragon and heat through. Season well with salt and pepper.

3 **onions**, chopped

2 **garlic cloves**, finely chopped

25 g (1 oz) **mixed nuts**, chopped

½ teaspoon **salt**

½ teaspoon **chilli powder**

¼ teaspoon powdered **saffron**

½ teaspoon grated **lemon rind**

2 teaspoons **anchovy paste**

3 tablespoons **vegetable oil**

750 g (1½ lb) peeled **prawns**

75 g (3 oz) finely shredded **coconut**

450 ml (¾ pint) **milk**

15

PREP

10

COOK

4

SERVES

spicy

Spicy prawn sauce

Prawns take on other flavours extremely well, which is why they often feature in curry dishes. In this recipe they are combined with chilli powder and coconut for a creamy pasta sauce with a bit of a kick. This sauce is best served with vermicelli or spaghettini.

1 Put the onions, garlic, nuts, salt, chilli, saffron, lemon zest and anchovy paste in a blender and purée until smooth.

2 Heat the oil in a frying pan, and gently fry the mixture for 3 minutes, stirring it constantly. Stir in the prawns, and fry for 2 minutes, until cooked.

3 Add the coconut and milk, bring to the boil and simmer for 1 minute.

Prawn, tomato and mushroom sauce

This quick and easy recipe is great for impromptu dinner parties as you can use large frozen, defrosted prawns, if necessary. Serve with spaghetti or, for a more unusual dish, some linguine verde.

1 Heat the oil in a large frying pan until almost smoking. Add the mushrooms and stir-fry for 2 minutes. Add the prawns and sun-dried tomatoes and stir-fry for another 3 minutes.

2 Add the lemon juice and spring onions, and stir-fry for another 2 minutes. Stir in the basil and season to taste with salt and pepper.

10 PREP

10 COOK

4 SERVES

quick

8 tablespoons **olive oil**

375 g (12 oz) **button mushrooms**, sliced

375 g (12 oz) large **prawns**, peeled and deveined

40 g (1½ oz) **sun-dried tomatoes** in oil, drained and chopped

2 tablespoons **lemon juice**

1 bunch of **spring onions**, diagonally sliced

3 tablespoons chopped **basil**

salt and **pepper**

½ teaspoon **saffron** threads

1½ tablespoons **tomato purée**

250 ml (8 fl oz) hot **water**

25 g (1 oz) **raisins**

8 tablespoons **olive oil**

½ small **onion**, finely chopped

1 **fennel bulb**, finely chopped

1 **garlic clove**, finely chopped

½ teaspoon **fennel seeds**, toasted and crushed

6 **anchovy fillets** in oil, drained and chopped

500 g (1 lb) fresh **sardines**, filleted

40 g (1½ oz) toasted **pine nuts**

pepper

4 tablespoons toasted **breadcrumbs**, to serve

30

PREP

20

COOK

4

SERVES

tasty

Saffron sardine sauce

Sardines are a real staple in Mediterranean cuisine but we tend to ignore them or just pull them out of the cupboard occasionally to adorn a piece of toast. They are packed full of essential oils and add a great flavour to sauces. Ask your fishmonger to fillet them.

1 Combine the saffron, tomato purée and the hot water, and set aside.

2 Soak the raisins for 15 minutes in enough hot water to cover them, then drain and roughly chop them.

3 Heat the oil in a large pan, and gently fry the onion and fennel until just soft. Add the garlic, fennel seed and anchovies. Fry for 1–2 minutes, mashing the anchovies to a paste.

4 Add the sardines and fry briefly on each side. Stir in the pine nuts, raisins, saffron solution and pepper. Bring to the boil, then reduce the heat and simmer over a medium heat for 5–7 minutes until the liquid reduces and the sardines break up a little. Serve hot with the breadcrumbs.

Tuna sauce

5
PREP

10
COOK

4
SERVES

rich

You can substitute the canned tuna for fresh tuna in this recipe and break it into larger flakes for a more chunky, substantial sauce. Just grill or pan-fry the equivalent amount of tuna until cooked through, then add it to the other ingredients.

1 Heat the oil and butter in a frying pan, add the garlic and cook over a moderate heat for 2 minutes. Pour in the stock and sherry, bring to the boil, then boil rapidly for 5 minutes to reduce the liquid.

2 Stir in the tuna, cream and two-thirds of the parsley. Season to taste with salt and pepper and stir well to mix. Garnish with the remaining parsley.

2 tablespoons **olive oil**

25 g (1 oz) **butter**

1 **garlic clove**, finely chopped

200 ml (7 fl oz) **fish stock** or **chicken stock** (see pages 18 or 19)

3 tablespoons **dry sherry**

200 g (7 oz) can **tuna**, drained and flaked

2 tablespoons **single cream**

3 tablespoons chopped **parsley**

salt and **pepper**

125 ml (4 fl oz) **olive oil**

1 **garlic clove**, crushed

250 g (8 oz) **mushrooms**, finely sliced

1 small **red pepper**, cored, deseeded and thinly sliced

200 g (7 oz) can **tuna** in oil, flaked but not drained

salt and **pepper**

finely chopped **parsley** or **basil**, to garnish

10

PREP

10

COOK

4

SERVES

easy

Tuna and mushroom sauce

This quick recipe is an ideal mid-week meal solution. The oil from the tuna is added to the dish to give it extra flavour. Serve with penne or macaroni.

1 Heat the olive oil in a frying pan and gently fry the garlic, mushrooms and pepper for 5 minutes, until the vegetables are tender but still firm.

2 Add the tuna to the pan and stir gently until the sauce is blended and heated through. Season to taste with salt and pepper, then garnish with chopped parsley or basil.

Sea bass and tomato sauce

15

PREP

30

COOK

4

SERVES

simple

2 **garlic cloves**

1 tablespoon **olive oil**

¼ teaspoon crushed **dried red chillies**

700 g (1 lb 6 oz) ripe **tomatoes**, skinned (see page 16) and roughly chopped

125 ml (4 fl oz) dry **white wine**

300 g (10 oz) skinned **sea bass** fillet, cut into thin strips

1½ tablespoons roughly chopped **flat leaf parsley**

extra virgin **olive oil**, for drizzling (optional)

salt

The better quality the ingredients you use, the less you need to do with them, and this pasta dish is a case in point. Use beautifully sweet, ripe tomatoes and the freshest sea bass for this simple yet impressive first course.

1 Place the flat side of a large cook's knife on the garlic cloves and press down firmly to bruise them. Heat the olive oil in a large frying pan over a low heat. Stir in the garlic and chillies and cook, stirring occasionally, for 10 minutes. If the garlic begins to colour, simply remove the pan from the hob and let the flavours infuse in the heat of the pan, then remove the garlic.

2 Stir the tomatoes and their juice into the infused oil and pour in the white wine. Season lightly with salt, bring to the boil and cook over a medium heat for 12–15 minutes until thickened.

3 Stir the fish and parsley into the sauce and cook for about 2 minutes until the fish turns opaque. Add a ladleful of hot water if the sauce appears too thick. Serve at once with a drizzle of extra virgin olive oil, if you like.

½ teaspoon **saffron** threads

375 g (12 oz) **monkfish** fillet

25 g (1 oz) **butter**

1 **fennel bulb**, finely chopped

1 teaspoon **fennel seeds**, crushed

250 g (8 oz) **mascarpone cheese**

splash of **white wine**

salt and **pepper**

10
PREP

15
COOK

4
SERVES

rich

Monkfish and mascarpone sauce

Monkfish is a great fish for tossing with pasta because it holds its shape very well. This rich, creamy sauce is particularly good with fresh pasta.

1 Crumble the saffron threads into 2 tablespoons just-boiled water in a small dish and leave to stand while you prepare the sauce.

2 Pat the fish dry on kitchen paper and cut away any bone and dark areas of the flesh. Thinly slice the fish and season lightly with salt and pepper.

3 Melt the butter in a frying pan and gently fry the monkfish for 2 minutes or until it is opaque. Lift out with a slotted spoon and add the fennel and seeds to the pan. Fry gently for 5 minutes or until softened.

4 Add the mascarpone to the pan with the saffron, the soaking liquid and wine and cook, stirring, until the cheese is melted and bubbling. Stir in the monkfish and cook gently for 2–3 minutes until cooked through. Season with salt and pepper to taste.

Asparagus and smoked salmon sauce

5 PREP

Smoked salmon and asparagus are a classic combination, and the distinctive flavours need little else to accompany them. This is a creamy sauce, which is best served with tagliatelle or fettuccine pasta.

8 COOK

175 g (6 oz) **asparagus** tips

125 g (4 oz) **smoked salmon**, cut into thin strips

300 ml (½ pint) **double cream**

1 tablespoon chopped **tarragon**

salt and **pepper**

Parmesan cheese shavings, to serve (optional)

1 Blanch the asparagus tips in lightly salted boiling water for 5 minutes. Drain under cold running water and pat dry.

2 Put the asparagus, smoked salmon, cream and tarragon in a saucepan and warm gently until heated through. Season to taste with salt and pepper, then serve with Parmesan shavings, if using.

4 SERVES

quick

300 ml (½ pint) **crème fraîche**

125 ml (4 fl oz) **vodka**

2 **spring onions**, finely chopped (optional)

1 teaspoon finely chopped **dill**, plus extra for garnish

250 g (8 oz) **smoked salmon**, cut into strips

salt and **pepper**

5

PREP

5

COOK

4

SERVES

simple

Smoked salmon and vodka sauce

This is another really quick sauce. The creamy element is supplied by crème fraîche, which has a slightly sour flavour – perfect with smoked salmon.

1 Pour the crème fraîche and vodka into a saucepan and heat gently until the mixture is almost boiling.

2 Add the spring onions, if using, and dill and cook until heated through. Season to taste with salt and pepper.

3 Remove the saucepan from the heat and stir in the smoked salmon. Garnish with the extra dill.

Smoked salmon, ginger and lime sauce

Savoury butters are utterly delicious when they melt into hot food, and this aromatic salmon butter is no exception. Cover and chill for up to 3 days until ready to use.

10

PREP

0

COOK

4

SERVES

exotic

100 g (3½ oz) **smoked salmon** slices or trimmings, finely chopped

100 g (3½ oz) **unsalted butter**, softened

25 g (1 oz) fresh **root ginger**, peeled and grated

finely grated **rind of 1 lime**, plus 1 tablespoon **lime juice**

2 tablespoons finely chopped **parsley** or **chervil**

pepper

lime wedges, to serve

1 Put all the ingredients in a bowl and beat well until evenly combined. Season with plenty of pepper.

2 Serve with the extra lime wedges for squeezing over the top of the pasta sauce.

25 g (1 oz) **butter**

1 **fennel bulb**, finely chopped

2 small **courgettes**, diced

2 **garlic cloves**, crushed

100 ml (3½ fl oz) **white wine**

100 g (3½ oz) fresh or frozen **peas**

small handful of chopped **dill**

250 g (8 oz) **mascarpone cheese**

150 g (5 oz) **smoked salmon** slices, cut into pieces, or trimmings

salt and **pepper**

10
PREP

15
COOK

4
SERVES

herby

Smoked salmon and dill sauce

Sauces provide a perfect use for packs of smoked salmon trimmings, which are very cheap but taste just as good as the more expensive choice pieces. Conveniently, the trimmings are also the right size for stirring into a delicious pasta sauce.

1 Melt the butter in a large saucepan and fry the fennel and courgettes very gently for 6–8 minutes until soft but not browned. Add the garlic and fry for 2 minutes.

2 Add the wine and a little salt and pepper and bring to the boil. Let the sauce bubble for a minute until the wine is slightly reduced.

3 Transfer the sauce to a food processor or blender and blend very lightly until it is pulpy but not smooth.

4 Tip the sauce back into the saucepan and add the peas, dill, mascarpone and salmon. Cook gently until heated through. Check the seasoning, then serve.

Herbed salmon sauce

15

PREP

15

COOK

4

SERVES

fresh

The herbs in this sauce result in a really fresh, summery flavour. The salmon is cubed rather than flaked, so it keeps its shape, rather than dissolving into the sauce. Serve with spinach fettuccine or tagliatelle.

1 Heat the oil and butter in a pan and gently fry the salmon for 3 minutes. Add the onions and fry for 1 minute more. Season to taste with salt and pepper. Remove the mixture from the pan with the juices and keep warm.

2 Add the wine, bring to the boil, then reduce the heat and simmer until reduced by half. Add the fish stock, return to the boil, then simmer to reduce by half again.

3 Stir in the cream and herbs, return to the boil, then simmer until the sauce is thickened and reduced. Gently stir in the salmon and onions and check the seasoning.

1 tablespoon **olive oil**

25 g (1 oz) **butter**

375 g (12 oz) boneless, skinless **salmon**, cut into 1 cm (½ inch) cubes

4 **spring onions**, green parts included, finely sliced

50 ml (2 fl oz) dry **white wine**

125 ml (4 fl oz) **fish stock** (see page 18)

500 ml (17 fl oz) **double cream**

3 tablespoons finely chopped fresh **coriander**

1 tablespoon each finely chopped **mint**, **rocket** and **lovage**

salt and **pepper**

1 kg (2 lb) fresh **mussels**, scrubbed and bearded (see page 176)

4 slices of fresh **root ginger**, plus 2 tablespoons finely shredded

2 **shallots**, finely chopped

2 **garlic cloves**, finely chopped

125 ml (4 fl oz) dry **white wine**

1½ tablespoons **olive oil**

25 g (1 oz) **unsalted butter**

250 g (8 oz) large **prawns**, peeled and deveined

250 g (8 oz) small **scallops**

125 ml (4 fl oz) **double cream**

1–2 teaspoons **lemon juice**

salt and **pepper**

deep-fried **basil leaves**, to garnish

30
PREP

15
COOK

6
SERVES

zingy

Marinara sauce with ginger

Fresh root ginger adds an oriental flavour to this delicious seafood pasta. It makes an ideal dish for an informal dinner party and is best served with tagliarini.

1 Place the mussels in a steamer. Scatter with the ginger slices, shallots and half of the garlic and sprinkle with the wine. Cover and steam over a medium-high heat for about 5 minutes until the mussels open.

2 Discard the ginger slices. Remove the mussels, discarding any that have not opened. Pour the cooking juices, shallots and garlic into a small saucepan. Cook over a high heat until the liquid is reduced to 125 ml (4 fl oz). Cover and set aside.

3 Heat a wok over a moderate heat. When it is hot, add the oil and butter, the remaining garlic and the shredded ginger and sauté for 30 seconds until softened.

4 Add the prawns and sauté for 1 minute until they begin to turn pink. Add the scallops and toss to mix. Pour in the reserved cooking juices and the cream and cook for 1 minute until the sauce becomes creamy.

5 Add the reserved mussels and lemon juice and season to taste with salt and pepper. Garnish with deep-fried basil.

Seafood medley sauce

This luxurious dish should be saved for special occasions. If halibut is unavailable, you could substitute other firm, white fish.

1 Melt the butter in a heavy-based saucepan, add the onion and garlic and cook gently, stirring, for 2 minutes. Add the flour and stir over a low heat for 2 minutes.

2 Gradually add the stock and the white wine and bring to the boil, stirring or whisking constantly until thickened.

3 Reduce the heat and stir in the halibut and scallops. Cook gently for 2–3 minutes.

4 Stir in the mussels, prawns, marjoram and cream, heat gently for 1 minute, then season to taste with salt and pepper.

15
PREP

10
COOK

4
SERVES

posh

50 g (2 oz) **butter**

1 **onion**, finely chopped

1 **garlic clove**, crushed

50 g (2 oz) **plain flour**

450 ml (¾ pint) **fish stock** or **vegetable stock** (see page 18 or 21)

150 ml (¼ pint) **white wine**

125 g (4 oz) **halibut**, cubed

6 **scallops**, cut into quarters

50 g (2 oz) canned or frozen **mussels**

125 g (4 oz) cooked peeled **prawns**

1 tablespoon chopped **marjoram**

150 ml (¼ pint) **single cream**

salt and **pepper**

50 g (2 oz) **butter**

1 **onion**, finely chopped

1 **garlic clove**, crushed

50 g (2 oz) **plain flour**

450 ml (¾ pint) **vegetable stock** (see page 21)

150 ml (¼ pint) **white wine**

125 g (4 oz) **monkfish**, cubed

6 **scallops**, cut into quarters

50 g (2 oz) **crab meat**

125 g (4 oz) cooked peeled **prawns**

1 tablespoon chopped **marjoram**

150 ml (¼ pint) **single cream**

salt and **pepper**

15

PREP

10

COOK

4

SERVES

rich

Mixed seafood sauce

Ring the changes on the Seafood Medley Sauce (see page 201) to include monkfish and crab meat. Serve with a small, shaped pasta such as conchiglie or orecchiette.

1 Melt the butter in a large, heavy-based saucepan, add the onion and garlic and cook gently, stirring, for 2 minutes. Add the flour and stir over a low heat for 2 minutes.

2 Gradually add the stock and the white wine and bring to the boil, stirring or whisking constantly until thickened.

3 Reduce the heat and stir in the monkfish and scallops. Cook gently for 2–3 minutes.

4 Stir in the crab meat, prawns, marjoram and cream, heat gently for 1 minute, then season to taste with salt and pepper.

Seafood and chilli sauce

This is another quick dish that would be perfect for a relaxed dinner with friends. Black tagliolini would make an impressive pasta accompaniment.

1 Heat the oil in a large frying pan and gently fry the pepper until just soft. Add the garlic and chillies and fry until the garlic starts to change colour.

2 Add the parsley, then the seafood, and stir-fry for about 5 minutes until heated through. Season to taste with salt and pepper.

10
PREP

10
COOK

4
SERVES

simple

8 tablespoons **olive oil**

1 **red pepper**, cored, deseeded and diced

2 **garlic cloves**, finely chopped

2 **red chillies**, deseeded and chopped

2 tablespoons chopped **flat leaf parsley**

750 g (1½ lb) **mixed seafood cocktail**

salt and **pepper**

1 small **onion**, finely chopped

2 **garlic cloves**, finely chopped

1 small **red pepper**, cored, deseeded and diced

1 small **green pepper**, cored, deseeded and diced

400 g (13 oz) can **chopped tomatoes**

4 tablespoons finely chopped **flat leaf parsley**

500 g (1 lb) **cod**, cubed

salt and **pepper**

PREP 10

COOK 15

Mediterranean fish sauce

Any firm white fish could be used in this recipe. It will soak up the juices and flavours of the sauce. Serve with rigatoni or penne.

4

SERVES

gutsy

1 Heat a frying pan and dry-fry the onion, garlic and peppers for 3–6 minutes, turning constantly, until soft.

2 Stir in the tomatoes, parsley and fish. Bring to the boil, then reduce the heat and simmer, uncovered, until the fish is just tender. Season to taste with salt and pepper.

Prawn and anchovy sauce

30
PREP

20
COOK

4
SERVES

rustic

Try using some large white anchovy fillets, if you can find them. Popular throughout the Mediterranean, they are slightly less salty than the darker variety. A good homemade fish stock will make all the difference to this delicious recipe.

1 Soak the anchovies in the milk for 15 minutes to reduce the saltiness. Drain the anchovies, chop and set aside.

2 Melt the butter in a saucepan, add the onion and cook for 10 minutes, stirring, until golden-brown. Add the garlic and cook for 1 minute.

3 Add the wine, bring to the boil and cook rapidly until reduced by half. Add the fish stock, anchovies and prawns and cook, uncovered, for 2 minutes.

4 Remove the pan from the heat and stir in the parsley. Season to taste with salt and pepper, then garnish with anchovy fillets and whole prawns.

10 **anchovy fillets** in oil, drained, plus extra to garnish

2–3 tablespoons **milk**

15 g (½ oz) **butter**

1 large **onion**, chopped

2 **garlic cloves**, thinly sliced

150 ml (¼ pint) dry **white wine**

250 ml (8 fl oz) **fish stock** (see page 18)

175 g (6 oz) cooked peeled **prawns**

2–3 tablespoons chopped **parsley**

salt and **pepper**

cooked unpeeled **prawns**, to garnish

1 **garlic clove**, chopped

200 g (7 oz) can **tuna** in brine, drained and coarsely flaked

3 tablespoons chopped **parsley**

2 tablespoons **tomato purée**

250 ml (8 fl oz) **fish stock** (see page 18)

salt and **pepper**

10

PREP

25

COOK

2

SERVES

thick

Tuna and tomato sauce

This is a great standby if you've got some fish stock in the freezer. The ingredients are reduced down substantially, which results in a wonderfully rich, thick sauce.

1 Heat a large frying pan or wok and dry-fry the garlic for 3–6 minutes, turning constantly, until it is soft and just beginning to colour.

2 Add the tuna, 2 tablespoons of the parsley, the tomato purée and fish stock. Bring to the boil, then reduce the heat and simmer gently for 15 minutes. Season to taste with salt and pepper, then sprinkle with the remaining chopped parsley.

Spicy puttanesca sauce

This variation on a traditional Italian dish (see page 45) includes red chilli for extra flavour. It is hot, spicy and very satisfying.

1 Heat the oil in a large saucepan. Add the onion and fry gently for 3–4 minutes until softened. Add the garlic and chilli and cook for a further minute.

2 Add the anchovies, tomatoes, sugar and olives, and bring to the boil. Reduce the heat and simmer gently for 10 minutes until the sauce is thick.

3 Add the basil, capers and a little salt and stir through for 1 minute. Serve at once, sprinkled with grated Parmesan, if liked.

15
PREP

15
COOK

4
SERVES

spicy

4 tablespoons **olive oil**

1 **onion**, finely chopped

3 **garlic cloves**, crushed

1 small **red chilli**, deseeded and finely chopped

6 **anchovy fillets** in oil, drained and chopped

2 x 400 g (13 oz) cans **chopped tomatoes**

½ teaspoon **caster sugar**

75 g (3 oz) **black olives**, pitted and finely chopped

small handful of **basil leaves**

2 tablespoons **capers** in brine, drained and rinsed

salt

freshly grated **Parmesan cheese**, to serve (optional)

1 **red pepper**

4 tablespoons **olive oil**

2 **garlic cloves**, finely chopped

6 **tomatoes**, skinned (see page 16) and chopped

50 g (2 oz) can **anchovy fillets** in oil, drained and finely chopped

4 tablespoons dry **white wine**

1 teaspoon **demerara sugar**

pepper

chopped **parsley**, to garnish

freshly grated **Parmesan cheese**, to serve

5
PREP

30
COOK

4
SERVES

rustic

Pepper and anchovy sauce

The saltiness of the anchovies is balanced out by the addition of demerara sugar and fresh parsley. This thick sauce needs a big pasta shape to complement it: rigatoni is perfect.

1 Grill the pepper under a preheated hot grill, turning occasionally, until it is blistered and charred on all sides. Place in a plastic bag and leave until cool enough to handle. Strip off the skin and chop the flesh.

2 Heat the oil in a large saucepan, add the chopped pepper and garlic and cook, stirring, for about 3 minutes. Add the tomatoes, anchovies, wine and sugar and season with some pepper.

3 Bring to the boil, then reduce the heat and simmer for 15–20 minutes until the sauce has thickened. Garnish with parsley and serve with grated Parmesan.

Mushroom and anchovy sauce

As this is quite a delicate sauce, make sure you buy the tiniest white button mushrooms that you can find. Larger, darker mushrooms will discolour the sauce and could spoil its pretty appearance.

1 Melt the butter with the oil in a large saucepan. Add the mushrooms and garlic and fry over a moderate heat, stirring constantly, for 5 minutes until the juices flow from the mushrooms.

2 Add the anchovies and cook for a further 5 minutes. Remove the pan from the heat and stir in 4 tablespoons of the parsley and the soured cream. Season to taste with pepper and sprinkle with the remaining parsley.

10

PREP

10

COOK

4

SERVES

easy

25 g (1 oz) **butter**

2 tablespoons **olive oil**

500 g (1 lb) tiny white **button mushrooms**

2 **garlic cloves**, crushed

1 50 g (2 oz) can **anchovy fillets** in oil, drained and roughly chopped

6 tablespoons chopped **parsley**

300 ml (½ pint) **soured cream**

pepper

cheese

25 g (1 oz) **butter**

75 g (3 oz) **pine nuts**

2 **garlic cloves**, thinly sliced

1 **leek**, finely shredded

300 ml (½ pint) **single cream**

finely grated **rind and juice of 1 lemon**

150 g (5 oz) firm **goats' cheese**, crumbled

salt and **pepper**

10

PREP

5

COOK

4

SERVES

quick

Goats' cheese and pine nut sauce

For a quick and easy, meat-free supper with plenty of texture and flavour, this sauce is difficult to beat and needs nothing more than a leafy herb salad to accompany it. Try it with fresh egg or spinach pasta.

1 Melt the butter in a frying pan and gently fry the pine nuts for about 2 minutes until they are beginning to colour. Add the garlic and leek and fry for another minute.

2 Add the cream, lemon rind and juice and goats' cheese to the pan. Season with a little salt and pepper and stir for 1–2 minutes until the cream is bubbling and the cheese has started to melt.

Rocket and goats' cheese pesto

Goats' cheese, rocket and hazelnuts replace pecorino, basil and pine nuts in this unusual pesto sauce. It has a rich, creamy flavour and a vibrant colour and would work well with linguine or spaghetti.

1 Place the rocket, hazelnuts, Parmesan and yogurt in a food processor or blender and process until almost smooth.

2 Stir in the goats' cheese and season to taste with pepper.

10

PREP

0

COOK

4

SERVES

rich

125 g (4 oz) **rocket**

40 g (1½ oz) toasted **hazelnuts**

40 g (1½ oz) **Parmesan cheese**, freshly grated

3 tablespoons natural **yogurt**

100 g (3½ oz) **goats' cheese**, chopped

pepper

50 g (2 oz) toasted **pine nuts**, plus extra to garnish

1 **garlic clove**, roughly chopped

150 g (5 oz) **watercress**

7 tablespoons extra virgin **olive oil**

150 g (5 oz) crumbly **goats' cheese**, plus extra to serve

salt and **pepper**

10

PREP

0

COOK

4

SERVES

fresh

Goats' cheese and watercress pesto

This twist on the classic basil pesto uses watercress and goats' cheese in place of basil and Parmesan. Be careful not to overblend the watercress and pine nuts in the food processor because the pesto is best when it still retains some texture.

1 Place the pine nuts, garlic and watercress in a food processor with a generous pinch of salt. Blend for 15 seconds until roughly chopped, then blend for another 20 seconds while drizzling in the olive oil.

2 Crumble in the goats' cheese and stir the pesto thoroughly. Season with pepper. Garnish with the extra pine nuts and serve with the extra goats' cheese.

Ricotta and spinach sauce

5
PREP

0
COOK

4
SERVES

simple

Ricotta is an extremely versatile soft cheese that is used with equal enthusiasm in sweet and savoury dishes. This simple sauce combines the cheese with spinach for a deliciously quick meal.

50 g (2 oz) **butter**

250 g (8 oz) frozen **spinach**, thawed and chopped

125 g (4 oz) **ricotta cheese** or **curd cheese**

50 g (2 oz) **Parmesan cheese**, freshly grated

salt and **pepper**

1 Melt the butter in a large frying pan, add the spinach and toss thoroughly. Season generously with salt and pepper and then sauté the spinach for about 2 minutes, stirring constantly.

2 Stir in the ricotta or curd cheese and half of the Parmesan, heat through and serve with the remaining Parmesan.

2 tablespoons **walnut oil**

2 **garlic cloves**, crushed

100 g (3½ oz) **walnut pieces**, chopped

150 g (5 oz) **dolcelatte cheese**

200 ml (7 fl oz) **crème fraîche**

2 tablespoons chopped **flat leaf parsley**

salt and **pepper**

10

PREP

5

COOK

3–4

SERVES

nutty

Creamy walnut and dolcelatte sauce

Walnuts make a great pasta sauce as they provide plenty of texture and flavour without the need for many other ingredients. This simple sauce is very rich, so serve it in small portions with penne or pasta twists and a tomato or leafy salad accompaniment.

1 Heat the oil in a frying pan and gently fry the garlic for 1 minute. Add the walnuts and fry for a further minute.

2 Crumble the cheese into the garlic and walnuts, then spoon in the crème fraîche and parsley. Add a little salt and pepper to taste, and heat for 1–2 minutes until the cheese is melting but still retains some texture.

Garlic, Parmesan and ciabatta sauce

This recipe provides a great use for ciabatta bread that's past its best, revitalized in a quick fry-up with olive oil, garlic, lemon, tomatoes and Parmesan.

1 Break the ciabatta into pieces, leaving the crust on, and blend lightly in a food processor to form very coarse crumbs.

2 Heat half the oil in a frying pan. Add the breadcrumbs and garlic and fry gently for 1–2 minutes, stirring, until pale golden.

3 Add the lemon rind and juice, tomatoes, Parmesan, the remaining oil and plenty of salt and pepper. Heat through for 30 seconds.

10
PREP

3
COOK

4
SERVES

rustic

150 g (5 oz) stale **ciabatta**

8 tablespoons extra virgin **olive oil**

2 **garlic cloves**, thinly sliced

finely grated **rind and juice of 1 lemon**

125 g (4 oz) **sun-blush tomatoes**, chopped

75 g (3 oz) **Parmesan cheese**, freshly grated

salt and **pepper**

3 tablespoons **olive oil**

2 **garlic cloves**, crushed

125 g (4 oz) **walnut pieces**

2 **plum tomatoes**, cut into wedges

50 g (2 oz) **Camembert cheese**, diced

50 g (2 oz) **Gruyère cheese**, freshly grated

1 bunch of **chives**, snipped

salt

10

PREP

15

COOK

4

SERVES

rich

Walnut, camembert and Gruyère sauce

This is a really rich, pungent sauce and this dish could be served in smaller quantities for a starter. Serve with penne or use spaghetti and twist a forkful into the centre of each plate for an attractive presentation.

1 Heat the oil in a large saucepan, add the garlic, walnuts and tomatoes and fry, stirring, for 1 minute. Reduce the heat.

2 Add both cheeses to the sauce, followed by all except 2 tablespoons of the snipped chives. Serve garnished with the remaining chives.

Mushroom and Gruyère sauce

Cheese and mushrooms are combined in many dishes, and this particular mix of exotic chanterelles and punchy Gruyère is a real treat. The cream works to dilute the cheese and thicken the sauce.

10

PREP

15

COOK

4

SERVES

thick

50 g (2 oz) **butter**

25 g (1 oz) **plain flour**

450 ml (¾ pint) **milk**

75 g (3 oz) **Gruyère cheese**, grated

250 g (8 oz) **button mushrooms**, finely chopped

125 g (4 oz) **chanterelle mushrooms**, finely chopped

2 **garlic cloves**, crushed

4 tablespoons **double cream**

salt and **pepper**

flat leaf parsley, to garnish

1 Melt half of the butter in a heavy-based saucepan. Add the flour and cook gently for 1 minute. Add the milk gradually, whisking or beating the sauce over moderate heat until thickened. Stir in the Gruyère and season to taste with salt and pepper. Set aside.

2 Melt the remaining butter in a large saucepan. Add the mushrooms and garlic and fry over a low heat for 5 minutes until the mushrooms have cooked down.

3 Add the Gruyère sauce to the mushroom mixture. Stir in the cream and cook gently over a low heat for about 2 minutes until thoroughly heated. Check the seasoning and garnish with parsley.

250 g (8 oz) **spinach**, tough stalks discarded

½ tablespoon **olive oil**

2 **garlic cloves**, crushed

¼ teaspoon grated **nutmeg**

300 ml (½ pint) **single cream**

250 g (8 oz) **mascarpone cheese**

salt and **pepper**

toasted flaked **almonds**, to garnish

15

PREP

10

COOK

4

SERVES

subtle

Spinach cheese sauce

Baby leaf spinach has smaller leaves and no stalks and it can be substituted here, if you prefer. Try this sauce with fresh wholemeal fusilli, or other short, ridged pasta.

1 Place the spinach in a large saucepan with just the water that clings to the leaves. Cook for 5 minutes or until the leaves have wilted. Remove from the heat, drain the spinach well and squeeze it to remove all the excess water. Chop finely and set aside.

2 Heat the oil in a large saucepan and fry the garlic over a low heat for 2 minutes until softened. Stir in the nutmeg, cream and mascarpone and season to taste with salt and pepper. Raise the heat and bring to just below boiling point.

3 Add the spinach, stir and cook gently for 1 minute. Garnish with toasted flaked almonds and serve immediately.

Cheesy egg and cream sauce

Although this is a no-cook sauce, it actually cooks once combined with the pasta. Add the cooked, drained pasta – tagliatelle is a good choice – to the pan and gently reheat the pasta and sauce, stirring carefully.

1 Beat the egg yolks in a saucepan. Add the cream, butter, salt, pepper and cheese and mix well.

5

PREP

0

COOK

4

SERVES

easy

8 **egg yolks**

142 ml (5 fl oz) **double cream**

125 g (4 oz) **butter**, cut into very small pieces

1 teaspoon **salt**

1½ teaspoons **pepper**

50 g (2 oz) **Parmesan cheese**, grated

25 g (1 oz) **butter**

250 g (8 oz) **Gorgonzola cheese**, crumbled

150 ml (¼ pint) **double cream**

2 tablespoons **dry vermouth**

1 teaspoon **cornflour**

2 tablespoons chopped **sage leaves**, plus whole leaves to garnish

salt and **pepper**

Gorgonzola sauce

PREP

COOK

SERVES

rich

Gorgonzola is a creamy yellow semi-soft cheese, with characteristic blue-green veins and a rich flavour. It was first produced over a thousand years ago in a village in the north of Italy called Gorgonzola.

1 Melt the butter in a heavy-based saucepan. Sprinkle in the crumbled Gorgonzola and stir it over a very gentle heat for 2 minutes until the cheese has melted.

2 Add the cream, vermouth and cornflour, whisking well to amalgamate. Stir in the sage. Cook, whisking all the time, until the sauce boils and thickens. Season to taste with salt and pepper and garnish with sage leaves.

Mascarpone and walnut sauce

This is another really quick and easy sauce that celebrates the combination of creamy mascarpone and crunchy walnuts. Serve with farfalle or conchiglie.

5

PREP

5

COOK

4

SERVES

quick

25 g (1 oz) **butter**

375 g (12 oz) **mascarpone cheese**

50 g (2 oz) **Parmesan cheese**, freshly grated

100 g (4 oz) shelled **walnuts**, coarsely chopped

1 tablespoon snipped **chives**

salt and **pepper**

1 Melt the butter in a saucepan. Add the mascarpone and heat very gently, without boiling, until melted.

2 Add the Parmesan, walnuts and chives and heat through. Season to taste with salt and pepper.

2 tablespoons mild **olive oil**

pared **rind of 1 lemon**, in thin strips

2 **garlic cloves**, thinly sliced

1 **red chilli**, deseeded and thinly sliced

2 teaspoons chopped **thyme**, plus a little extra to garnish

100 g (3½ oz) **cream cheese**

2 tablespoons **vodka**

1 tablespoon **lemon juice**

salt

2 tablespoons toasted flaked **almonds**, to garnish

10
PREP

5
COOK

2
SERVES

spicy

Cheesy lemon and vodka sauce

This spicy sauce, enlivened with chilli and vodka, might be the answer when you fancy a quick and easy lunch or supper to perk up jaded taste buds. It is really good served with fresh linguine or vermicelli.

1 Heat the oil in a saucepan and add the lemon rind, garlic, chilli and thyme. Fry gently for about 2–3 minutes or until the ingredients start to colour.

2 Add the cream cheese to the saucepan and heat through gently until it softens to the consistency of pouring cream. Stir in the vodka, lemon juice and a little salt. Garnish with toasted almonds and the extra thyme.

Mushroom and herby cheese sauce

Mushrooms, white wine and cheese make a fresh-tasting sauce that's great for easy entertaining. Serve with spinach tagliatelle for an extra splash of colour and flavour.

1 Heat the oil in a saucepan and fry the onion and garlic until softened. Add half the chives with the mushrooms and wine.

2 Bring to the boil and cook for 2 minutes, then remove from the heat, stir in the cheese and cream and season to taste with salt and pepper. Stir until heated through, then garnish with the remaining chives.

10 PREP

10 COOK

4 SERVES

herby

1 tablespoon **olive oil**

1 **onion**, chopped

2 **garlic cloves**, crushed

2 tablespoons snipped **chives**

250 g (8 oz) **button mushrooms**, sliced

125 ml (4 fl oz) dry **white wine**

50 g (2 oz) **herby cheese roule with pepper**

125 ml (4 fl oz) **double cream**

salt and **pepper**

25 g (1 oz) **butter**

1 **onion**, chopped

2–3 **garlic cloves**, crushed

125 g (4 oz) **streaky bacon**, rind removed and diced

75 g (3 oz) **Bel Paese cheese**, freshly grated

75 g (3 oz) mature **Cheddar cheese**, freshly grated

75 g (3 oz) **Gruyère cheese**, freshly grated

50 g (2 oz) **Parmesan cheese**, freshly grated

300 ml (½ pint) **double cream**

2 tablespoons chopped **parsley**

2 tablespoons chopped **chives**

1 tablespoon chopped **basil**

5

PREP

10

COOK

6

SERVES

rich

Four-cheese sauce

Streaky bacon adds a wonderful smoky flavour to this pungent cheese sauce. It's important that all the cheeses are freshly grated and the herbs are freshly chopped to make the most of the flavours.

1 Melt the butter in a saucepan. Add the onion and garlic and cook gently, without browning, for about 2–3 minutes. Add the bacon and cook for a further 5 minutes, stirring occasionally.

2 Stir in the cheeses and cream, ensuring the cheeses melt, followed by the herbs.

Broccoli and blue cheese sauce

Broccoli and blue cheese make a fantastic combination in this simple but delicious pasta sauce. It's ready in no time and would be great for an after-work treat. Try accompanying the sauce with wholewheat conchiglie.

5 PREP

5 COOK

250 g (8 oz) **broccoli**, cut into small florets

125 g (4 oz) **blue cheese**

50 g (2 oz) **butter**

125 ml (4 fl oz) **double cream** or **crème fraîche**

salt and **pepper**

1 Cook the broccoli florets in lightly salted boiling water for 3 minutes until just tender. Drain well and keep warm.

2 Put the saucepan back on the heat and add the blue cheese, butter and cream or crème fraîche. Heat gently, stirring all the time to make a smooth sauce. Check the seasoning and add salt and pepper if necessary.

3 Return the broccoli to the pan and toss thoroughly to mix with the sauce.

4 SERVES

easy

200 g (7 oz) **basil leaves**, plus sprigs to garnish

175 ml (6 fl oz) **olive oil**

75 g (3 oz) **pine nuts**

4 **garlic cloves**, chopped

175 g (6 oz) **Parmesan cheese**, freshly grated

25 g (1 oz) **Cheddar cheese**, freshly grated

50 g (2 oz) **ricotta cheese**

50 g (2 oz) **butter**, softened

salt

10
PREP

0
COOK

4–6
SERVES

simple

Three-cheese pesto

This is another sauce that will 'cook' once the pasta is added. It can be prepared in advance and then simply stirred into the cooked, drained pasta and combined over a low heat, until the cheese melts and warms through.

1 Put the basil leaves, oil, pine nuts and garlic in an electric blender or food processor and work until smooth.

2 Transfer to a bowl and stir in the cheeses and salt to taste. Beat in the butter, then add 1 tablespoon hot water to slacken the sauce. Garnish with basil sprigs.

Dolcelatte cheese sauce

PREP 5

The rich, creamy taste of dolcelatte is allowed centre stage in this simple sauce. Choose a good-quality cheese and serve with fresh tagliatelle for the ultimate in fast food.

COOK 5

1 Melt the butter in a heavy-based saucepan. Add the cheese and melt over a very low heat.

2 Gradually stir in the cream, beating it vigorously with a wooden spoon so it blends into the cheese. Remove the pan from the heat, stir in the sage and add pepper to taste. Garnish with whole sage leaves.

SERVES 4

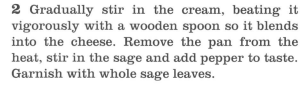

rich

25 g (1 oz) **butter**

175 g (6 oz) **dolcelatte cheese**, diced

150 ml (¼ pint) **double cream**

2 teaspoons finely chopped **sage leaves**, plus whole leaves to garnish

pepper

quick and easy

400 g (13 oz) **dried spaghetti** or other long thin pasta

2 tablespoons **olive oil**

1 **onion**, finely chopped

200 g (7 oz) **pancetta**, cut into cubes

2 **garlic cloves**, finely chopped

3 **eggs**

4 tablespoons freshly grated **Parmesan cheese**

3 tablespoons chopped **flat leaf parsley**

3 tablespoons **single cream**

salt and **pepper**

10

PREP

10

COOK

4

SERVES

classic

Quick carbonara sauce

This super-quick sauce should be enough to persuade everyone away from jars. Green salad goes well with creamy carbonara.

1 Cook the pasta in a saucepan of boiling salted water for 8–10 minutes or according to the packet instructions until al dente.

2 Meanwhile, heat the oil in a large, non-stick frying pan. Add the onion and fry until soft. Add the pancetta and garlic and cook gently for 4–5 minutes.

3 Beat the eggs with the Parmesan, parsley and cream. Season to taste with salt and pepper and set aside.

4 Drain the pasta and add it to the onion and pancetta. Stir over a gentle heat until combined, then pour in the egg mixture. Stir and remove the pan from the heat. Continue mixing well for a few seconds, until the eggs are lightly cooked and creamy.

Chicken liver and sage sauce

Chicken livers have a smooth, creamy texture like no other meat. Serve with a tomato salad or plenty of crispy leaves in a fresh, tangy dressing. This sauce is particularly good with herb- or black pepper-flavoured fresh tagliatelle.

1 Rinse the chicken livers and thoroughly dry on kitchen paper. Cut into small pieces, discarding any white, fatty parts.

2 Heat the oil in a large frying pan. Add the whole sage leaves and fry quickly for 30 seconds until crisp. Remove with a slotted spoon and pat dry on kitchen paper to remove the excess oil.

3 Add the butter to the pan and fry the shallots for 3 minutes until softened. Stir in the garlic and chicken livers and fry gently, stirring, for a further 2–3 minutes or until the livers are lightly browned but still slightly pink in the centre.

4 Stir in the Marsala, cream and shredded sage leaves and heat through gently until bubbling. Season to taste with salt and pepper and garnish with fried sage leaves.

10
PREP

10
COOK

4
SERVES

rustic

500 g (1 lb) fresh **chicken livers**

3 tablespoons **olive oil**

20 **sage leaves**, 8 shredded and 12 left whole to garnish

25 g (1 oz) **butter**

2 **shallots**, finely chopped

2 **garlic cloves**, crushed

4 tablespoons **Marsala wine**

3 tablespoons **single cream**

salt and **pepper**

2 tablespoons **olive oil**

1 **onion**, thinly sliced

400 g (13 oz) can red or pink **salmon**

150 g (5 oz) frozen **peas**

2 tablespoons **pesto**

1 tablespoon **lemon juice**

25 g (1 oz) **Parmesan cheese**, freshly grated, plus shavings to garnish

salt and **pepper**

10
PREP

3
COOK

4
SERVES

quick

Pesto salmon sauce

Canned salmon might not taste as good as its fresh counterpart, but it is ideal for creating an easy meal in minutes. Bottled pesto sauce is another valuable store-cupboard standby. Use either green or red pesto, which is flavoured with peppers and tomatoes.

1 Heat the oil in a frying pan, add the onion and fry for about 5 minutes until softened. Drain the salmon and discard any skin and bones. Roughly flake the flesh with a fork.

2 Cook the peas in lightly salted water for 3 minutes. Drain, retaining a few tablespoonfuls of the cooking water, and add to the frying pan.

3 Stir in the pesto, lemon juice, Parmesan, onion and flaked salmon. Season lightly with salt and pepper and toss gently. Serve with Parmesan shavings.

Prosciutto and pea sauce

10
PREP

10
COOK

If peas are in season substitute fresh for the frozen peas in this recipe. They will take a little longer to cook but will add that extra fresh flavour. Serve the sauce with conchiglie or gnocchi.

1 Melt the butter in a pan, add the prosciutto and gently fry for 1–2 minutes until lightly browned.

2 Add the petit pois and spring onions and fry for 2–3 minutes

3 Pour in the cream and season lightly. Bring to the boil, then reduce the heat and simmer over a medium-high heat, stirring constantly, until the sauce has thickened. Stir in the Parmesan.

4
SERVES

easy

50 g (2 oz) **butter**

250 g (8 oz) **prosciutto**, diced

300 g (10 oz) frozen **petit pois**, thawed

6 **spring onions**, green parts included, finely sliced

300 ml (½ pint) **whipping cream**

salt and **pepper**

50 g (2 oz) **Parmesan cheese**, freshly grated

3 tablespoons **olive oil**

8 **sun-dried tomatoes** in olive oil, drained and chopped

1 **garlic clove**, crushed

125 g (4 oz) **button mushrooms**, sliced

125 g (4 oz) rindless **back bacon**, grilled

salt and **pepper**

4 large **sage leaves**, torn, to garnish

10

PREP

3

COOK

4

SERVES

rich

Mushroom, bacon and tomato sauce

The combination of sun-dried tomatoes and crispy bacon gives this sauce a lovely, rich flavour. Serve with spirale pasta.

1 Heat the oil in a large saucepan and fry the sun-dried tomatoes, garlic and mushrooms for 2 minutes, stirring constantly.

2 Crumble in the grilled bacon and heat for 1 minute. Season to taste with salt and pepper and serve with sage leaves.

Garlic and chilli sauce

With just four ingredients, this pasta sauce couldn't be simpler to prepare. It is typical of the no-nonsense Italian approach to food. Choose spaghetti for this sauce.

1 Heat the oil in a frying pan, add the garlic and chilli and fry for 1–2 minutes.

2 Add the parsley and season to taste with black pepper.

10

PREP

2

COOK

4

SERVES

simple

2 tablespoons **olive oil**

4 **garlic cloves**, finely chopped

1 **red chilli**, deseeded and chopped

2 tablespoons chopped **parsley**

pepper

125 ml (4 fl oz) **olive oil**

½ teaspoon **ground ginger**

pinch of freshly grated **nutmeg**

1 **garlic clove**, crushed

3 tablespoons **capers** in brine, drained and rinsed

75 g (3 oz) pitted **black olives**, sliced

2 tablespoons chopped **parsley**

salt and **pepper**

sprigs of **basil**, to garnish

10

PREP

2

COOK

4

SERVES

spicy

Spicy olive sauce

Capers are a great alternative to anchovies in vegetarian sauces because they also have an intense, salty flavour. This sauce has a good texture so would work well with penne.

1 Heat the oil in a saucepan and add the ginger, nutmeg, garlic, capers, olives and chopped parsley.

2 Season to taste with salt and pepper and stir over a low heat for 1–2 minutes. Garnish with basil sprigs.

Creamy vodka and tomato sauce

The vodka gives this creamy pasta sauce a distinctive kick, making it a real winner. There's quite a lot of Parmesan here but it helps to bind the pasta and sauce.

5

PREP

2

COOK

6

SERVES

tasty

50 g (2 oz) **butter**

6 tablespoons **tomato purée**

450 ml (¾ pint) **single cream**

9 tablespoons **vodka**

salt and **pepper**

1 tablespoon chopped **basil**, to garnish

6 tablespoons freshly grated **Parmesan cheese**, to serve

1 Melt the butter in a saucepan over a low heat and stir in the tomato purée and cream.

2 Take the pan off the heat and add the vodka and a little salt and pepper. Garnish with basil and serve with Parmesan.

10 tablespoons **olive oil**

8 **spring onions**, green parts included, finely chopped

finely grated **rind of 1 lemon**

75 g (3 oz) trimmed **mixed fresh herbs**, such as flat leaf parsley, rocket, thyme, marjoram, basil, rosemary, chopped

salt and **pepper**

TO SERVE:

4 tablespoons toasted **breadcrumbs**

50 g (2 oz) **Parmesan cheese**, freshly grated

10

PREP

2

COOK

4

SERVES

zingy

Fresh herb and lemon sauce

This is a real summer dish and just needs a simple tomato and onion salad to complete the meal. Fresh herbs are packed full of flavour so there's really no need for other ingredients. This sauce is best served with farfalle or fusilli pasta.

1 Heat the oil until it is very hot. Remove from the heat and immediately stir in the spring onions, lemon rind and herbs.

2 Season generously with salt and pepper, then serve hot with the breadcrumbs and Parmesan cheese.

Citrus crème fraîche sauce

PREP 5

This light, fresh sauce uses lemon rind and juice for a real citrus kick. Serve with fresh tagliatelle verdi for a colourful lunch dish.

COOK 5

1 Place the crème fraîche in a saucepan with the lemon rind and juice. Stir over a very low heat until the crème fraîche becomes creamy.

2 Stir in the chopped parsley, season to taste with salt and pepper, and garnish with lemon rind and parsley sprigs.

SERVES 4

light

250 g (8 oz) **crème fraîche**

1 tablespoon **grated lemon rind**

1 tablespoon **lemon juice**

2 tablespoons chopped **parsley**

salt and **pepper**

TO GARNISH:

strips of **lemon rind**

sprigs of **parsley**

1 large bunch of **basil**

75 g (3 oz) toasted **pine nuts**

1 **garlic clove**

75 g (3 oz) **Parmesan cheese**, freshly grated

grated **rind of 2 lemons**

4 tablespoons **lemon juice**

3 tablespoons **olive oil**

salt and **pepper**

Lemon pesto

5

PREP

0

COOK

This fresh-tasting pasta sauce uses very few ingredients but has a very full flavour. It's so quick and easy to prepare that it's ideal for any occasion.

4

SERVES

1 Place all of the ingredients in a food processor or blender and process them until smooth. Season to taste with salt and pepper.

fresh

Burnt sage butter sauce

Burnt butter tastes fantastic and is one of the simplest things to make, although the timing is absolutely crucial. You need to brown the butter only a little, so once you see it turning, throw in the lemon juice to stop it cooking any further.

1 Heat the butter in a frying pan over a medium heat and add the pine nuts and sage. Stir until the nuts are light brown and the butter is pale golden.

2 Have the lemon juice to hand and, once the butter is pale golden, turn off the heat and quickly pour in the lemon juice.

3 Season the butter with salt and serve the sauce scattered with Parmesan shavings.

5

PREP

5

COOK

4

SERVES

herby

50 g (2 oz) **butter**

50 g (2 oz) **pine nuts**

15 **sage leaves**, sliced

2 tablespoons **lemon juice**

salt

freshly grated **Parmesan cheese**, to serve

2 tablespoons **olive oil**

2 large **leeks**, sliced

300 g (10 oz) **chestnut mushrooms** or **button mushrooms**, quartered

3 **garlic cloves**, crushed

2 tablespoons chopped **sage** (optional)

freshly grated **nutmeg**

4 tablespoons **double cream**

1 teaspoon **cornflour**

200 g (7 oz) **Greek yogurt**

100 g (3½ oz) **sprouted mung beans**

salt and **pepper**

10
PREP

7
COOK

4
SERVES

light

Leek and mushroom sauce

This yogurt-based sauce is much lighter than typical rich, creamy pasta sauces and has a refreshing tang. Sprouted beans add colour, texture and plenty of nutrients, but you may prefer to add a scattering of sunflower seeds, pine nuts or toasted almonds instead.

1 Heat the oil in a large frying pan. Add the leeks, mushrooms, garlic, sage, if using, plenty of nutmeg and a little salt and pepper. Fry gently for 5 minutes.

2 In a bowl, mix the cream and cornflour to a smooth paste, then stir in the yogurt

3 Add the yogurt mixture and sprouted beans to the leek mixture, along with a few tablespoons of hot water, and heat through gently for 2 minutes; do not allow to boil or the sauce may curdle.

Walnut and pine nut sauce

This sauce has a rough texture and a toasted, nutty flavour that is complemented by the butter and cheese.

1 Toast the walnuts lightly under a pre-heated grill, then remove the skins. Chop finely along with the pine nuts and garlic (or put them in a blender or food processor).

2 Melt the butter in a saucepan, add the chopped nut mixture and cook on a medium heat until golden. Season with salt and pepper, remove from the heat and stir in the Parmesan. Pour in the cream and mix well. Return to the heat just to warm through.

10
PREP

10
COOK

4
SERVES

nutty

250 g (8 oz) **walnuts**, shelled

1 teaspoon **pine nuts**

2 **garlic cloves**

50 g (2 oz) **butter**

25 g (1 oz) **Parmesan cheese**, freshly grated

250 ml (8 fl oz) **single cream**

salt and **pepper**

500 g (1 lb) **broccoli** florets

dried chilli flakes, to taste

50 g (2 oz) **butter**

100 g (4 oz) **Parmesan cheese**, freshly grated

salt and **pepper**

10

PREP

3

COOK

4

SERVES

simple

Broccoli and chilli sauce

Broccoli is packed full of iron so this is a great recipe for vegetarians who need to ensure they eat plenty of green vegetables. The chilli adds a good, fiery finish, without detracting from the main ingredient.

1 Cook the broccoli florets in lightly salted boiling water for 3 minutes until just tender. Drain and break into smaller pieces and dice the stalks. Place in a bowl.

2 Add the chilli flakes, butter and half the Parmesan. Mix well, adding a little water if necessary to keep the mixture moist. Season to taste with salt and pepper. Serve with the remaining grated Parmesan.

Rocket and cherry tomato sauce

This quick sauce uses peppery rocket as if it were spinach, stirred into garlicky sweet cherry tomatoes until wilted, then seasoned with balsamic vinegar.

10

PREP

2

COOK

4

SERVES

quick

1 Heat the oil in a frying pan, add the garlic and cook for about 1 minute until golden. Add the tomatoes and cook for barely 1 minute. They should only just heat through and start to disintegrate.

2 Sprinkle the tomatoes with the balsamic vinegar, allow it to evaporate, then toss in the rocket. Carefully stir to mix it in and heat through so that the rocket is just wilted. Season to taste with salt and pepper. Serve with plenty of Parmesan shavings.

3 tablespoons **olive oil**

2 **garlic cloves**, finely chopped

500 g (1 lb) very ripe **cherry tomatoes**, halved

1 tablespoon **balsamic vinegar**

175 g (6 oz) **rocket**

salt and **pepper**

Parmesan cheese shavings, to serve

2 teaspoons **olive oil**

2 **onions**, finely chopped

8 **courgettes**, thinly sliced

1 tablespoon freshly grated **Parmesan cheese**

salt

10

PREP

10

COOK

4

SERVES

simple

Courgette sauce

If courgette flowers are available, they can be washed, sliced and added to the courgettes and onion while they are frying. They have a very delicate flavour.

1 Heat the oil in a large frying pan, add the onions and fry gently for about 5 minutes until soft and transparent.

2 Add the courgettes after 3 minutes and fry them gently until just tender, stirring frequently to prevent them from sticking. Cover the pan if the courgettes start to burn on the outside before they are cooked through. Add salt to taste.

3 Carefully add a ladleful of hot water and the Parmesan and stir to form a moist, creamy sauce.

Blue cheese sauce

Blue cheese has such a wonderfully dominant flavour that there's really no point trying to let other ingredients battle it out. Butter and cream add the liquid element to the sauce and, best of all, it's ready in minutes.

1 Crumble the cheese into a small saucepan and add the butter and cream.

2 Cook over a low heat to melt the cheese and warm the mixture. Season to taste with pepper.

5

PREP

2

COOK

4

SERVES

cheesy

300 g (10 oz) **Gorgonzola cheese** or **dolcelatte cheese**

75 g (3 oz) **butter**

150 ml (¼ pint) **double cream**

pepper

3 tablespoons **olive oil**

25 g (1 oz) **butter**

½ **onion**, chopped

1 small **carrot**, finely sliced

1 **celery stick**, sliced

125 g (4 oz) **Italian sausage**, skinned and crumbled

½ small **yellow pepper**, cored, deseeded and diced

4 **basil leaves**, torn, plus extra whole leaves to garnish

50 ml (2 fl oz) dry **red wine**

TO SERVE:

2 tablespoons freshly grated **pecorino cheese**

2 tablespoons freshly grated **Parmesan cheese**

10
PREP

10
COOK

4
SERVES

hearty

Sausage and vegetable sauce

Italian sausage adds a really intense flavour to this hearty vegetable-based sauce, while the combination of pecorino and Parmesan cheeses adds a rich, creamy topping to the finished dish.

1 Heat the oil and butter in a flameproof casserole, add the onion, carrot and celery and cook over a low heat for 4 minutes.

2 Add the sausage, pepper and basil and mix well. Cook over a moderate heat for 3–4 minutes until the sausage has browned. Add the red wine. Garnish with basil leaves and serve with both grated cheeses.

Peperoni condiverdi sauce

This sauce could also be used as a pizza or bruschetta topping. It's a handy one for a store-cupboard meal as there are just a few ingredients. Serve with spaghetti and some fresh, crusty bread.

1 Heat the oil in a saucepan and add the pepper, antipasto and parsley. Stir well.

2 Heat gently for about 1 minute or until thoroughly warmed through. Add salt to taste and serve with Parmesan shavings.

5

PREP

2

COOK

4

SERVES

rustic

6 tablespoons **olive oil**

1 teaspoon **pepper**

285 g (9½ oz) jar **antipasto peperoni condiverdi**

2 tablespoons chopped **parsley**

salt

125 g (4 oz) **Parmesan cheese**, shaved, to serve

index

a

Executive Editor Nicky Hill

Editor Leanne Bryan

Executive Art Editor Darren Southern

Designer Ginny Zeal

Senior Production Controller Martin Croshaw

Introduction supplied by Cara Frost-Sharratt